FINDING HOPE
IN THE DARKNESS

Devotions for Those Who Grieve

Karen Pilarowski

Finding Hope in the Darkness

Copyright © 2021 by Karen Pilarowski.

ISBN: 978-1-63357-383-3

All rights reserved.

Unless otherwise indicated, all Scripture quotations are taken from THE HOLY BIBLE, NEW INTERNATIONAL VERSION®, NIV® Copyright © 1973, 1978, 1984, 2011 by Biblica, Inc.® Used by permission. All rights reserved worldwide.

Scripture quotations marked "ESV" are taken from The Holy Bible, English Standard Version. Copyright © 2000; 2001 by Crossway Bibles, a division of Good News Publishers. Used by permission. All rights reserved.

Scripture quotations marked "MSG" are taken from The Message. Copyright 1993, 1994, 1995, 1996, 2000, 2001, 2002. Used by permission of NavPress Publishing Group.

Illustrations by Naomi Miller/Winding Lane Studio

Dedicated To

Mark

Save a place for me next to you

Acknowledgements

A humble Thank You to:

The many friends and family who surrounded me with love after Mark's death

Sue Wengerd who first believed in my book and Phil Barkman who did a wonderful job of editing

Naomi Miller who not only created the beautiful illustrations, but also kept me lifted in prayer during the difficult times

Mike Nash who gave me unconditional support and enthusiasm

Ginger Taddeo who kept me alive during the greatest trial of my life. You are my sister, my friend, my forever family. I thank you and I thank God for you.

Contents

FINDING HOPE IN THE DARKNESS

Introduction

Mark and I married on May 21, 1983. It was far from a fairy-tale love story.

I actually had become a Christian through the pain of a broken engagement to another man. Recently graduated from college, I could not find a job; my father had been given a year to live, and then my fiancé decided he really didn't love me after all. I remember sitting in a bathtub with the water running so no one could hear my disconsolate sobs. My life felt over before it ever began. A failure at life and a failure at love, I wanted to die. I paged through a Bible I had been given while still on campus. Flipping the pages with my tears falling into my bathwater, my eyes fell on this verse: "See what great love the Father has lavished on us, that we should be called children of God!" (1 John 3:1).

My tears stopped immediately. Only the Spirit of God knows why that verse spoke to my broken heart and wounded soul the way it did. It is another evidence of how the Word of God is living and active and changes lives. Instead of seeing FAILURE in bright, flashing neon letters above my head, I saw LOVE. And not just love, but great love, lavished love, love by the God of the universe who called Himself my Father and called me His child. Love that could never be taken away.

I realized, in that precious, crystalline moment, that no matter what was taken away from me in this world—success, family, love, anything and everything—I could *never* lose the love of God.

To say it changed my life would be an understatement.

Mark was part of a singles fellowship at a large church I began attending after my engagement crashed and burned. He was a nice guy, tall and thin, with a beard and a great smile that engaged anyone who met him. He also had a laugh that could coax the grumpiest, sour-pickle-eatingest person in the world to grin. It was unique and contagious. And it was constant. He was a goofy guy and could make me laugh like no one else in the world. We shared similar interests and became friends. And that's how it was for about six years.

I dated other guys but remained close friends with Mark. After another long-term relationship disintegrated, Mark was there to encourage me, to make me laugh, to help me move on. But we were just friends.

Mark went to a Bible college in England, and I began corresponding with him. I told him of all the hometown happenings, kept him informed of all the latest engagements, and encouraged his pursuit of God. Little did I realize that while in England, he was discussing life and relationships with a very godly man who was convincing him that a godly wife was more precious than jewels.

Mark returned from England, and we continued our friendship. However, things began to change. I am not even sure how or when, but we began to think of each other as more than friends. Neither of us let on to the other that our feelings were changing. Then one day, during a walk, Mark confessed his love for me and asked me to marry him. I told him I would pray about it and get back to him. I then went out and bought a Bride's magazine.

The next day I said, "Yes."

Our marriage was definitely not perfect. We both had issues that needed to be dealt with, and sometimes it felt like the struggle was not worth it. But we were joined in covenantal marriage, and we were committed to making it work.

In many ways, Mark was the perfect match for me. Our senses of humor were totally in sync, and we made each other laugh until we couldn't breathe. He had spiritual insights that often surprised me. He respected my intellect and encouraged me in my creative endeavors.

Because we both had come from exceptionally small families and never had children, we developed a special bond. Due to our very similar interests, we did almost everything together. Over the course of the years, we developed a comfortable life. We made plans for our retirement in 2019 and looked forward to traveling the country.

I made reservations for a cruise for our thirty-fifth wedding anniversary coming up in May of 2018. I did not get the cancellation insurance because our parents were now gone, and we were healthy; what could go wrong?

February 19, 2018, ended with a normal evening. Mark set his clothes out for the next day, and we retired to bed.

At about 4:00 am, I woke up because Mark was making some unusual noises. I asked him if he was all right, and he didn't answer. Knowing he was a very sound sleeper, I thought he was just having a bad dream. I got up to shower and get ready for work.

When I came out of the bathroom and turned on the light, I knew something was extremely wrong. Mark seemed to be flailing in bed and making guttural noises. When I went over to him, he could not respond to me. I called the ambulance. As they were taking him out of the house, the EMT's told me what I already had guessed. He was having a stroke.

I followed them to the hospital and began reviewing in my mind things that needed to be done. It would most likely be a long recuperation, but we could do it. I would research the best facilities. He might not have the abilities he once had, but with time and determination from both of us, we would make it. Yes, I might need to postpone my retirement because of finances and insurance, but we would make it. With God's help, we would make it.

Friends met me at the hospital. I was thankful they were there when the doctor told me Mark had had an ischemic stroke and might never be normal again. I remember the feeling of slowly sinking into deep water, of being unable to breathe, of thinking this could not be happening. Not to Mark. Not to me.

It was necessary to life flight him to another hospital where they could further diagnose the damage to his brain. It was during the flight that his fate was determined. He had another stroke, but this time it was hemorrhagic. They had to perform emergency surgery to remove part of his skull to allow for swelling from the bleeding. Half his brain was dead. Without the least bit of compassion, the doctor told me he would never walk, talk, feed himself, or possibly even survive.

When I next saw him, his head was swollen from the bleeding, but he looked very peaceful. As the nurses looked into his eyes, I realized Mark was no longer with me. Although his heart was beating, he was not there.

A more compassionate doctor suggested waiting forty-eight hours to see if there would be any reversal of his condition. Those two days are a blur. Family and friends surrounded us and made sure someone stayed with me at all times. We prayed for a miracle. After forty-eight hours, there was no longer any brain activity.

I wanted Mark to be free to be with his Savior. God was calling him home.

I stayed by his side, holding his hand, letting him know I would see him again. Letting him know I loved him. Letting him know I would not give up on God because of this.

The ventilator was removed. We waited in silence. His breathing slowed, then stopped.

Mark was with God.

I was alone.

My grief journey began. Although I knew God would be with me for the rest of my life and my friends would always support me, the feeling of aloneness was utterly overpowering. I had no idea I was even capable of surviving the deep, cutting pain that threatened to shatter my heart and soul. I didn't want to survive it.

But God said, "Live," and in obedience, I did.

At Mark's funeral, I spoke of my faith in God. I knew I needed to do this to honor Mark, but also to honor God. I had to speak confidently of my faith in God. It was all I had left.

Somehow, life continued. In those first few months, I am not exactly sure how. Friends and family made sure I took care of the necessary arrangements. They made sure I ate and moved. But eventually, everyone needed to resume their lives.

I would never "resume" my life. It had been irrevocably changed. I would never be the same person I was.

God still put the breath of life in me each day. I needed to use it. I joined an exercise class, attended a Bible study, and started both private and group grief counseling. I began journaling, and as I kept writing, the simple cries for mercy from a broken and shattered heart evolved into something more.

This book is the result of God reaching out to me in my grief and teaching me not only who He is, but how much more He loves me than I ever imagined. God truly has embraced me.

It is my heartfelt prayer that anyone suffering a loss can identify with the vulnerable, sorrowful cries from my grief. But more importantly, I hope they can see the immense, comforting, life-affirming love of God that does not change no matter what our circumstances.

God touches us in our joy and in our grief. Death separates us from our loved ones. But as I learned so many years ago, nothing can ever separate us from the love of God.

Still Here

I woke up on February 20, 2018, thinking it would be a normal day. Mark was making a lot of noise, and I could not figure out why. At the time, I had no clue he was having a stroke. Then came an ambulance, an ER, a life flight, surgery, and tears. More tears than I ever knew I was capable of. Then desperate prayers, sickening realizations, and final decisions. Two days later, my world changed forever. Mark was gone.

But I was still here, staring at his wedding ring given to me in a small, silken bag. I went through the robotic responses of a widow at a funeral. I tried not to think, because thinking terrified me. How could I live without him? How could I ever laugh again? No one would ever hold my hand. We would never vacation again. We would never travel in an RV and see the country as we had planned. A million horrible, gut-wrenching, breath-stealing thoughts flowed through my mind, an unrelenting torrent of fear and grief.

How could I survive? Mark was gone. How could I face the future? Mark was gone. How could I laugh, how could I ever smile again? Mark was gone. My world was gone. Who would take care of the yard like he did? Who would decorate cakes for friends? Who would make floral arrangements for me? Who would say, "I'm home, lovely wife," every night at 6:30?

The collateral damage is often not considered when a person dies. I not only lost a husband, but I also lost a repairman, a gardener, a cook, a nurse, a driver, a comedian, a dancer, a Sherpa, a friend. I lost someone who made life worth living. I lost everything.

Eventually, I heard a still, small voice within me: "Ah, but you didn't lose Me."

My life changed when Mark stopped breathing, but God remained the same. God was—and still is—my Protector, my Provider, my Rock, my Refuge, my Redeemer, and my Savior.

He did not change. But I did.

I need to seek God now, more than ever before. I sift through His Word, looking for comfort and hope. I pray that He gives me wisdom for day-to-day decisions I never had to make before. I reach to Him in the dark of night when I am alone and weeping.

He is there every time, waiting for me. He has always been there, waiting for me.

> *Be strong and courageous. Do not be afraid or terrified because of them, for the LORD your God goes with you; he will never leave you nor forsake you. (Deuteronomy 31:6)*

It is comforting to know that God never changes and that I *can* change. I will not be pulled into this quicksand of grief forever. I try to focus on the truth of God's Word and not my unreliable, undependable emotions. It is not easy, and sometimes reading a promise or reciting a Scripture cannot satisfy the yearning for the touch of my husband and the sound of his voice. I think God understands this. He made us relational people. He grieves by my side because death was never how He wanted life to end. But He also rejoices with Mark who is experiencing the joys of heaven right now. The joys I will experience one day.

God puts the breath of life in me each day. All He asks is that I live. To honor Mark and to worship God, I will. Today, I will live.

Tomorrow is in God's hands.

PRAYER

Lord, I will never understand Your reason for taking my husband. But I trust Your loving hand. I know You are in control, You are with me, and You have a plan for my life. Help me to live for You.

MEDITATION

You are my hiding place; you will protect me from trouble and surround me with songs of deliverance. (Psalm 32:7)

When anxiety was great within me, your consolation brought me joy. (Psalm 94:19)

thoughts to remember

FINDING HOPE IN THE DARKNESS

6

Tree of Life

I sat in my family room on an overcast, frigid day in February, gazing out my window. Snow covered the ground. The trees were barren. The world was mostly devoid of color. The world outside echoed my emotions since my husband had just died.

I focused on the tree across the street. While the pines around it were green, this tree had lost its leaves and stood exposed in the winter wind. My heart ached. I had been stripped of all that was meaningful in my life. I was barren and cold, shivering in the winds of grief. I could not imagine a future. I could not fathom seeing the sun again.

"Look at the tree," the Lord spoke to my heart. "You are that tree."

I felt God gently reminding me that I had entered a new season in my life. I could not see the future. I took no delight in the past. I only felt the icy fingers of pain and grief close around my heart.

> That person is like a tree planted by streams of water, which yields
> its fruit in season and whose leaf does not wither—whatever they do
> prospers. (Psalm 1:3)

Was I like the tree in Psalm 1? I wanted to delight myself in the Lord. I wanted to plant myself in His Word and find life there. But by myself, I simply was not capable. I could not get past my husband's death. I would never love again.

One day, the voice of the Lord said, "Patience." Mentally, I knew that spring would arrive and the barren tree outside would sprout leaves of green. The colorless landscape would explode with the brightness of trees and bushes and flowers. The sky would be blue, and the warm sun would shine.

But today, I could not see the hope of spring in my heart.

As I go through seasons in my life, there are days of darkness and despair, and it seems like I will never see light again. Then suddenly, there is a bud of hope in the distance, and I see future possibilities. I long for summer when I can fully turn my face to light and warmth again.

"Patience," the Lord whispers. "Patience."

I can't rush the seasons. They are out of my control. I just live in them when they change. When the barrenness of winter comes, I try to find warmth in the embrace of God's truths. When spring arrives, I try to thank God for hints of what is to come.

I long to be the tree whose leaf does not wither. I am firmly planted by the stream of God's love. I drink from it daily and try to wait patiently for the season of yielding fruit once again.

PRAYER

Lord, give me patience to withstand the changing seasons in my life. The stream of Your love sustains me, and I will one day be fruitful again.

MEDITATION

I am the vine; you are the branches. If you remain in me and I in you, you will bear much fruit; apart from me you can do nothing. (John 15:5)

So that you may live a life worthy of the Lord and please him in every way: bearing fruit in every good work, growing in the knowledge of God. (Colossians 1:10)

thoughts to remember

FINDING HOPE IN THE DARKNESS

Shaky Ground

The initial news of Mark's stroke rocked my world. An aura of unreality permeated every doctor's word, every hospital smell, every beat of my heart. My life was crumbling before my eyes, and I had no control over it.

I had seen footage of violent earthquakes. Furniture rattled, dishes fell out of cabinets, pictures crashed from the walls, buildings turned to dust. People were devastated. Many were left without homes. Some even died. Living in the Midwest, I had only experienced small earthquakes, but even then, the strength of the shaking ground was frightening. Furniture moved, windows vibrated. Even a tiny earthquake's impact was felt.

Now, I was going through one of life's most significant, life-shifting events. The ground was not moving, but it might as well have been. I felt as though I could not gain my footing. I watched helplessly as my world ended.

In physical earthquakes, survivors often say, "At least we have each other." I had been displaced, and I was now alone. I thought it would have been easier to go through an actual earthquake than this emotional one. Dishes and houses can be replaced. My husband could not.

> *God is our refuge and strength, an ever-present help in trouble. Therefore we will not fear, though the earth give way and the mountains fall into the heart of the sea. (Psalm 46:1–2)*

At Mark's funeral, I read a eulogy that included Psalm 46:1. My world had given away, and I had only God to cling to. It was the first verse I thought of when Mark died because I desperately needed refuge.

It is a verse I have clung to all my life because even when Mark was alive, he could not give me hope. Salvation is from the Lord, and my hope comes from the Lord. My soul grasped this truth and clung to it like the dying person I was. I sought refuge in the Lord because I could not bear the reality of life. I sought strength in the Lord because I was too weak to even breathe on my own.

In my heart, the earth had given way, the mountains had fallen, the seas were roaring, and the land quaked. But God was also in my heart, saying, "Peace." Just as in a physical earthquake, the violent shaking does not last forever, and my heart eventually calmed with the soothing words of God. He met me in Scripture, He met me in the comfort of friends, He met me in praise, He met me in the laughter of children. My life quieted, but the shaking did not stop as I experienced daily "griefquakes" that paralyzed my world and made me hang on to God. I expect the griefquakes will last the rest of my life, but hopefully, they will be less intense and spaced further apart.

When my world shakes with the immensity of my loss, there is nothing more I can do than cling to God. He has promised me a place of refuge.

PRAYER

Lord, let me find my refuge in You, whether the earth shakes or all is still. You are my refuge and strength.

MEDITATION

Cast your cares on the LORD and he will sustain you; he will never let the righteous be shaken. (Psalm 55:22)

For I am convinced that neither death nor life, neither angels nor demons, neither the present nor the future, nor any powers, neither height nor depth, nor anything else in all creation, will be able to separate us from the love of God that is in Christ Jesus our Lord. (Romans 8:38–39)

FINDING HOPE IN THE DARKNESS

thoughts to remember

FINDING HOPE IN THE DARKNESS

The Balm of Praise

In those first terrifyingly painful days of grief, I could do very little. My main goal for each day was: (1) Get out of bed, and, (2) Shower. Anything else was superfluous. I was in survival mode. I had to figure out life in the midst of a tsunami, an earthquake, and a volcanic eruption all at once. And through all these tragedies, I had to do it alone. That shower was a major accomplishment.

Of course, I had friends surrounding me, and I could not have survived without them. But at the end of the day, I had to climb the stairs alone and get into an empty bed and lay in the darkness. Alone.

My first cries to God were exactly that—cries. I had no words. I wailed, I screamed, I cried so hard I could barely find breath. I reached out my arms to God and felt no touch being returned. Eventually, the only word I could utter in prayer was, "Mercy."

This went on night after night. Even when the day seemed tolerable, the night wrapped its cold, suffocating arms around me and brought tears and wails and cries for mercy once again. I lifted my arms as a child does to her father, tearfully begging to be picked up and comforted. No comfort came. The nights were hellish.

One night, as I lifted my arms once again in supplication and uttered my tear-choked "Mercy," I realized I was also in a position of praise. How could I praise God now? He had taken my husband, my joy, my hopes, my dreams. Praise Him?

My life had been swept away, and where was God? Was He swallowed by the tsunami? Was He shattered by the earthquake? Was He destroyed by the volcano?

God was still God. He had not changed through all of my tragedies. He was still worthy of praise.

Seeing this truth, I offered a few words. I praised Him for who He is—Savior, Redeemer. Then came a few more. Protector, Provider. I knew that the only one able to lead me through the days and nights was God. My Rock. My Fortress. My Deliverer. He would be with me whether I felt his arms or not. Faithful. Eternal. Holy.

There began my realization of the balm of praise. Every night, I reached out to God and praised Him for who He is. Unchanging. An Anchor for my soul. I praised Him through the tears and found it calmed my spirit. When grief rose up and threatened to overtake me again, I praised God and found I was able to focus on the awesome character of God instead of the enormous depth of my grief.

It was not easy. The first few words came out through clamped teeth and clenched fists. But in my heart, I knew God never changes, and He is forever worthy of praise.

> *Jesus Christ is the same yesterday and today and forever. (Hebrews 13:8)*

He is forever worthy of praise, even when my world falls apart. Especially when my world falls apart, because it is only God who can put it back together. He was not surprised, and He has a plan for my future.

I learned very slowly about the healing power of praise. There is power in using the Bible to pray back to God the words He uses to describe Himself.

Praise is not optional in times of grief. It is the way through it.

PRAYER

Lord, help me to continue to reach out to You in praise as well as supplication. You never change and will be with me forever.

MEDITATION

God is not human, that he should lie, not a human being, that he should change his mind. Does he speak and then not act? Does he promise and not fulfill? (Numbers 23:19)

Every good and perfect gift is from above, coming down from the Father of the heavenly lights, who does not change like shifting shadows. (James 1:17)

thoughts to remember

FINDING HOPE IN THE DARKNESS

Darkness Into Light

There were times when my world was total darkness. The bottomless blackness of the initial shock was the worst. I saw no light and no way out. I wanted to die, simply to end the pain. Then came the fog of early grief. Perhaps it was not as dark as the shock, but it was still oppressive and foreboding. I was still trapped in darkness. I could not pray, and I could not focus on reading God's Word. I couldn't even care for myself. Without friends to help me during this time, I would still be stumbling in the fog. It lasted for months, and with eyes clouded by storms of tears, I thought it would never end.

Yet, I yearned for light. I didn't want to stay in the darkness, but it seemed like grief didn't want me to leave. When I thought I saw a glimmer of light, grief pulled me back.

Eventually, I managed to read a verse. It was all I could tolerate. Psalms have always been my favorite, and I slowly worked through them, one verse at a time. I took comfort in the pain expressed by the Psalmist. I was not alone in sorrow.

But how could a verse here or there truly help me get through the most horrific time of my life? I needed to climb out of this relentless black hole of grief. I knew I could not survive there. I needed light. I craved light. How could I find it?

It is common to feel abandoned by God in grief, to feel isolated and forsaken. Just because something is common does not make it hurt less. I know I was not the first to feel intense grief, nor would I be the last. But this grief was personal. I was not talking about someone else who lost a spouse. This was me. This was my reality.

I kept reading, even though there was no significant diminishing of the darkness. Was I an anomaly? Did God forget about me?

And then, there it was. It started as a tiny spot of brightness, a minute point of light that promised more. If I followed it, I knew I could find my way out of the darkness.

> *This is the message we have heard from him and declare to you: God is light; in him there is no darkness at all. (1 John 1:5)*

God's Word will never return void. I faithfully read His Word, believing that eventually the light would break through. I didn't feel differently, but God, the creator of light, promised there would *be* a difference. I kept on, reading a little more each day, searching in the darkness for any speck of light.

One day, the light broke through. It was a tiny sliver of brightness at first. I felt new purpose in each day. I was, after all, created for fellowship with God, and I was determined to seek Him.

Someday, I will be standing in the glorious light of His presence. I cannot imagine the beauty of that moment. Until then, I follow the light in His Word.

PRAYER

Lord, let me seek Your light daily. Don't let me dwell in the darkness, for it threatens me each day. Let me find the light of Your love.

MEDITATION

You, LORD, are my lamp; the LORD turns my darkness into light. (2 Samuel 22:29)

For with you is the fountain of life; in your light we see light. (Psalm 36:9)

thoughts to remember

FINDING HOPE IN THE DARKNESS

Digging for Treasure

I like watching shows on archeology. It is fascinating to watch archeologists with a new discovery. Each find generally requires a large hole or tunnel to be dug. They carefully dig out the treasure, sometimes tunneling deep within the earth to pull their artifact to light.

Grief has left a gaping hole in my heart. But, like the archeologists, I can't just bury it and move on. I need to tunnel deeper. Grief has made it possible to go deeper than ever before, exploring parts of me I never even knew existed. The treasure I am seeking is God. I know this tunnel in my heart could collapse at any time from the weight of the emotions I feel—fear, anxiety, sorrow, confusion, deep grief. I must continuously shore it up with the truth of God's Word.

It is only God's Word that sustains me through the lonely days and nights, the uncertainty of the future, the financial instability. As painful and frightening as it is, I dig deeper, often covered in tears and wailing in pain. I dig deeper, questioning my sanity in this pursuit, wondering if I should simply lie down and die instead of moving forward in this interminably long, dark tunnel. But then I see a sparkle, a glimmer of hope.

> *Praise be to the God and Father of our Lord Jesus Christ, the Father of compassion and the God of all comfort, who comforts us in all our troubles, so that we can comfort those in any trouble with the comfort we ourselves receive from God. (2 Corinthians 1:3–4)*

There is purpose to the pain. I understand, as I never have before, the promise in this verse as well as the direction.

It is not just buried treasure. It is living treasure, able to transform my life.

I must continue deeper into this cavern in my heart created by grief. It is God leading me forward into the unknown. But I must trust Him—I must!—to lead me to more and more shining treasures until, at last, I hear His loving, comforting voice: "Welcome home, my daughter. Welcome home."

It is one shovel at a time. Just as using dynamite to excavate a site could destroy the artifacts, so would plowing through this tunnel of grief destroy the supports and cause me to miss the treasures to be found. I need to move slowly, purposefully, examining each step. I need to sift through the dirt and be willing to dedicate time and resources to this task. I cannot sidestep the pain. It will not be easy, but it is necessary.

The treasure of God's Word awaits.

PRAYER

Lord, give me strength to withstand the pain and to move deeper to find Your comfort. I cannot do this journey alone. Light my way as I dig deeper. Guide me, support me, love me.

MEDITATION

Indeed, if you call out for insight and cry aloud for understanding, and if you look for it as for silver and search for it as for hidden treasure, then you will understand the fear of the LORD and find the knowledge of God. (Proverbs 2:3–5)

Every word of God is flawless; he is a shield to those who take refuge in him. (Proverbs 30:5)

thoughts to remember

I pray that, eventually, my twisted and choked heart will ease.

FINDING HOPE IN THE DARKNESS

Twisted Sheets

I looked at my bed after I awoke. I thought, "How could I have slept in that mess and survived?" The sheets were twisted like a fabric tornado, the blanket was knotted in a pile on the floor, and the pillow was pulled out of its case. It was a shocking sight, the remnants of a battle fought in my sleep. My husband had been right. I DID steal the covers every night.

As I looked at the remains of my bed, I also felt, once again, the deep pain of loss. Although the blankets and sheets were awry, Mark's pillow never moved. He was not here to move it.

How like my bed my life seems right now! When Mark was alive, everything felt in order. The days proceeded in a predictable manner. He had his responsibilities, and I had mine. I would dust, cook dinner, and pay bills. He would vacuum, wash dishes, and make the bed. We worked together to accomplish what needed to be done. Sometimes, even when I tried to help him put sheets on the mattress, he would tell me he would take care of it. He liked the corners tucked in a certain way, and I could not tuck as well as he could.

Suddenly, I found myself with not only my responsibilities but with his as well. The days fell out of order. I cried when I weeded the garden because I thought of him on his hands and knees, covered in dirt, happily working in his flowers. I cried when I had to change the water filter in the refrigerator because I could not figure out how to follow the instructions and remove it without turning it. I cried when I broke the filter. I think of him every time I take out the trash, or bring in the paper in the rain, or change the cat litter, or have to figure out why there is a weird noise in the basement.

My life is like that bed, twisted and disheveled and out of control. And Mark is not in it.

> *I can do all this through him who gives me strength. (Philippians 4:13)*

God will supply what I need to want to live again. He will give me the wisdom to know when I can't do something myself. Just as Mark and I split household duties, God does not expect me to shoulder the burdens by myself. I love the image of the body of Christ because I have experienced His hands and feet helping me paint, move furniture, and pull weeds.

God will also give me strength to look at that bed morning and night and see the pillow that hasn't moved.

I pray that, eventually, my twisted and choked heart will ease. I will learn to do what I must and acquire help for the things I cannot do. God will help me bring order to my life. But the sheets will always remain twisted.

PRAYER

Lord, everything in my life feels twisted right now. Help me to smooth my choked heart. Lead me to those who can help, and whenever possible, let me help others as well.

MEDITATION

The LORD gives strength to his people; the LORD blesses his people with peace. (Psalm 29:11)

Trust in the LORD with all your heart and lean not on your own understanding; in all your ways submit to him, and he will make your paths straight. (Proverbs 3:5-6)

thoughts to remember

FINDING HOPE IN THE DARKNESS

The Real Enemy

When reading through the Psalms, I never really dwelt on those that referred to enemies. After all, I thought, I have no enemies. I am generally friendly with most people, and my friends have been incredibly supportive and caring. I could not relate to verses like Psalm 31: 8: "You have not given me into the hands of the enemy but have set my feet in a spacious place." Then, it hit me. We have an enemy who will one day claim all of us for his own. We will succumb, no matter how hard we fight. The enemy is Death. We all have an expiration date, determined by God. No one can avoid it.

We hope to escape Death as long as possible. I thought my father died young at age seventy-two. But my mother lived to one month shy of age eighty-nine, and my aunt lived to age ninety-five. I thought I might have a chance of living long enough to celebrate fifty or sixty years of marriage. But then the enemy slipped in, completely unexpected and certainly unwanted, and claimed my husband. How could this be? Surely there was a mistake made. Did Death visit the wrong house? Was the wrong person taken? It didn't seem real.

We are all dying, although at different rates, some faster than others. In those first few weeks of intense, mind-numbing pain and the fog of deepest grief, I felt as though Death had won. Mark was gone and would never return. I was devastated, afraid, and brokenhearted. The enemy had triumphed. I also yearned for death. I thought of how even Jesus passed through the cold grip of death.

But then, that wasn't the end of the story, was it?

For we believe that Jesus died and rose again, and so we believe that God will bring with Jesus those who have fallen asleep in him. (1 Thessalonians 4:14)

Yes, Death is the enemy. It has been from Adam and will be until Jesus returns. Death was not God's perfect plan for mankind. God, in His redeeming nature, took what we had lost—eternal life—and gave it back to us through the death and resurrection of Jesus Christ. Yes, we will all die, but no, we will not be dead forever. Death has been reduced to a minor inconvenience, a stop on the way to God's eternal presence. We take our last breath and close our eyes to earth, but having accepted the gift of Christ's death as payment for our sins, we immediately open them to the Living God in heaven. Even our bodies, dead and decaying in the ground, will one day be resurrected to glorious life.

Of course, I was apprehensive about seeing Mark in a casket for the first time. My stomach was in knots, and I could not control my tears. But, as soon as I saw him, I was reminded that although his body may still be here awaiting a physical resurrection, his soul was resting in the loving arms of Jesus.

Mark professed his faith in Jesus Christ as a young adult and kept strong in his faith throughout the rest of his life. As one of God's mercies to me in those first pain-filled days, Mark had a smile on his face as he lay in the casket. It made me think that he, having fought the specter of Death, was now facing his Savior and would never again face the enemy. God had triumphed. Mark was home.

However, I still have life ahead of me. And that means someday standing face to face with the enemy, Death. I will lose the battle, but only temporarily. I know who wins the war. Just as Mark passed through the hands of Death, so will I. It will not hold me.

I hope there will be a smile on my face as I lie in my casket. But even if there is not, I can say with full confidence that Death will be defeated. I will stand in the presence of God and Mark, my place reserved by the blood of Jesus. Death, for me, will no longer have any power.

PRAYER

Lord, let me live the life You have chosen for me. Don't let Death defeat me while I still live. Give me hope for tomorrow.

MEDITATION

Very truly I tell you, whoever hears my word and believes him who sent me has eternal life and will not be judged but has crossed over from death to life. (John 5:24)

Jesus said to her, "I am the resurrection and the life. The one who believes in me will live, even though they die; and whoever lives by believing in me will never die. Do you believe this?" (John 11:25–26)

thoughts to remember

FINDING HOPE IN THE DARKNESS

FINDING HOPE IN THE DARKNESS

Two Feet On Earth,
One Heart In Heaven

I am living a divided life. I have two feet on earth, but one heart in heaven. As any person who has lost a spouse knows, I feel split in two. This tearing asunder has been described in many ways: amputation, pages once glued together now torn apart, a hole in the soul. Whatever the image, the feeling is the same. The two that were one no longer exist. Half of me is missing.

This shift in balance made me feel confused and directionless. I was going in circles, like a rudderless boat on choppy seas. I could not control the feelings of incompleteness that plagued my every thought. Part of me was missing. I cried and cried over my loss because I knew I would never feel that oneness again.

It was disconcerting to realize part of me is in heaven. I immediately wanted to learn all I could about paradise. I knew Mark was there, but *where* was there? What was he experiencing? Was he really happy?

The Bible promises eternity in heaven for those who believe in Jesus. It tells us it is beyond what we can imagine. I needed more. I needed to visualize the joys of heaven so I could be more at peace with my loss on earth. I read books on heaven, both fiction and non-fiction. I needed to know because, for this time, my existence on earth seemed like hell. I needed to know Mark was now experiencing the promises we had lived for.

I imagined his new life in heaven. While on earth, Mark loved to talk to people—friend or stranger, it didn't matter. In heaven, he could talk for eternity to those he had only dreamed of. After Jesus, I'm sure he made a beeline for his hero, George Washington. Then, the patriarchs of the faith: Moses, David, Paul. There are family and friends who went before him. So many conversations, so much time.

On earth, Mark loved gardening. I have no doubt the flowers in heaven are breathtaking. It must be wonderful to garden without toil, to see plants without thorns, and never to battle insects and disease.

Before Mark passed away, I sometimes thought of how wonderful heaven would be. Now that Mark is a citizen there, I think of it often. I yearn for it. I take comfort in knowing that I am promised it. My name is written in heaven, and I rejoice.

Of course, my thoughts of heaven are just that—thoughts. The Bible gives us examples of what heaven is like, but we must wait to have full knowledge and experience of it. Mark has that knowledge today. I must continue to live here on earth, longing for heaven, but living life as God calls me.

> *Praise be to the God and Father of our Lord Jesus Christ! In his great mercy he has given us new birth into a living hope through the resurrection of Jesus Christ from the dead, and into an inheritance that can never perish, spoil or fade. This inheritance is kept in heaven for you.*
> *(1 Peter 1:3–4)*

One day, the hole in my heart will be healed. I will no longer feel amputated or torn apart. The reunion with Mark will be very sweet, but being in the presence of my Savior even sweeter.

PRAYER

Lord, let me live each day with eternity in my heart. Even as I long for heaven, let my life on earth glorify You.

MEDITATION

For we know that if the earthly tent we live in is destroyed, we have a building from God, an eternal house in heaven, not built by human hands. (2 Corinthians 5:1)

Brothers and sisters, we do not want you to be uninformed about those who sleep in death, so that you do not grieve like the rest of mankind, who have no hope. (1 Thessalonians 4:13)

thoughts to remember

FINDING HOPE IN THE DARKNESS

To Be In His Presence

I had always been a person who enjoyed solitude. Life was too noisy, fragments of sound constantly circling me throughout the day. At work, there was the noise of conversations, radios playing, and meetings occurring—the distractions went on and on. After work, I craved quiet. I would come home, relax, and make dinner without a sound. We had subdued conversation at dinner, and then we would relax in the relative quiet.

After Mark died, I could not stand the silence. I had to have a TV on or the radio playing or some kind of music in the background. Without the noise, I would be able to think, and that is the last thing I wanted to do.

I could not sit quietly. I needed noise, any noise. I was thankful it was winter because my windows were closed, and my neighbors could not hear my wails of grief. I also needed to cry out to God, whether through tears or prayers or shouts. I became extremely vocal. I needed to know God saw me. I needed to know God heard me. I was drowning in a sea of sound, afraid to find an inlet of quiet.

This need for noise went on for many months. As soon as I entered my house, something was turned on, the louder the better. I had sound at home and sound in my car; I could barely tolerate pauses in conversations with friends. With quiet came tears.

Slowly, the TV went off for extended periods of time. Then the music. I could read once again because I did not have constant, distracting, background noise. I could praise the Lord quietly instead of at the top of my lungs. As time went on, I realized I no longer needed to cry out or shout for God's attention. I knew He heard me. I just wanted to be in His presence.

> *The LORD replied, "My Presence will go with you,*
> *and I will give you rest." (Exodus 33:14)*

Just be. He called me to Himself, gently and lovingly—the Lover of my soul. Just be, in holy silence, meditating on who He is and all He has done for me. Although the noise distracted me from my grief, it also distracted me from hearing the small, quiet voice of God.

Without words, without raging emotions, He calls me to just be in His presence, in the quiet, so He can whisper words of love to my heart. He draws me to Himself, and I rest.

The silence now is not filled with thoughts of despair. It is filled with the whispers of God—just being in His presence.

PRAYER

Lord, I just want to be in Your presence. Speak to me in the silence, and open my heart to hear You.

MEDITATION

You make known to me the path of life; you will fill me with joy in your presence, with eternal pleasures at your right hand. (Psalm 16:11)

Even though I walk through the darkest valley, I will fear no evil, for you are with me; your rod and your staff, they comfort me. (Psalm 23:4)

thoughts to remember

44

Holding Hands

For me, weekends are the worst. During the week, I can muster some distractions that keep me from continual tears. I go to the gym, I meet friends for lunch or dinner, or I do general errands that keep me moving. But on Saturday mornings, I open my eyes with dread for the day.

Saturdays were my favorite days. When I was working, I actually did a little Friday dance of joy for the coming weekend. I looked forward to sleeping in and spending time with my husband. Even if we just did chores around the house, it was a great feeling to accomplish tasks together. We would often go out to dinner or do a special activity, such as going to a museum. Wherever we went, we held hands. We always held hands no matter where we were or how we felt. It was our "thing."

While we were standing in line at the last event we attended together, a stranger commented, "Still in love after all those years." Mark smiled and said, "Thirty-four and still going." A few weeks later, I held his hand as he died.

I feel emptiness in every pore of my body, but my hand feels numb. I will never again feel his touch, his hand close around mine in reassurance. I remember all of the times our hands were together: walking on the Caribbean beaches on vacation, tightly clenched over each of our parents' graves, strolling through a park admiring the beautiful wildflowers, or sitting on the couch just watching TV. It was such a simple touch, but it meant the world to me.

I see couples walking hand-in-hand now, and I am crushed with grief. I walk alone. No one holds my hand. I look at it, and it is empty. No wedding ring adorns it. It feels as though everyone in the world has a hand-holding partner, and although I know that is not true, my eyes only focus on couples. My body aches with aloneness. Who will hold my hand again?

Yet I am always with you; you hold me by my right hand. (Psalm 73:23)

When I read that God holds my hand, I dissolved into tears. God is with me every step of this grief journey, and He will hold my hand through it.

There were times when Mark and I had a disagreement. I did not want to hold his hand, but he took it anyway. My hand lay in his like a dead fish. There have also been times I did not want the touch of the Lord. I did not want to walk this journey with Him. I wanted Mark back. But God held me fast and would not let me go. Even though I was unresponsive, God was patient and waited until I grasped His hand in return.

I will not walk this grief journey alone. God holds me by my right hand.

PRAYER

Lord, I know You walk with me. Forgive the times I want to run from You. Never let me go.

MEDITATION

If I go up to the heavens, you are there; if I make my bed in the depths, you are there. If I rise on the wings of the dawn, if I settle on the far side of the sea, even there your hand will guide me, your right hand will hold me fast. (Psalm 139:8–10)

For I am the LORD your God who takes hold of your right hand and says to you, Do not fear; I will help you. (Isaiah 41:13)

thoughts to remember

FINDING HOPE IN THE DARKNESS

Home Security

Everyone has their own personal fears. Some women do not like snakes—
I have handled a boa constrictor. Some women do not like heights—I have
gone rappelling. My quirky personal fear is having my picture taken. There
are many reasons why I have this fear, and I understand none of them make
sense. It may seem like a silly, frivolous fear to have, but it has been there for
many years and has only increased as I have aged.

When I was at an outdoor concert the other night, someone took a picture of me. It suddenly hit me that I no longer had Mark for protection. He
had been my picture guard, and nothing was snapped without my expressed
approval. Now the guard was gone.

One of the first things I did after Mark died was to have a security system installed in the house. I never felt unsafe here, but suddenly, I was alone.
I felt like easy prey, even though the police blotters generally recorded only
public drunkenness or minor vandalism. But I no longer had someone at
night I could jab in the ribs and whisper, "I heard a noise."

Mark protected me in more than home security. He did things purely for
my comfort. When I slept in, he closed the curtain so the light would not
wake me. He brought me a glass of water every morning because I woke
up so thirsty. He started the coffee. He shielded my eyes and turned off the
sound to TV commercials for horror movies because he knew I would have
nightmares.

Knowing that I HATED having my picture taken, he would never pressure me to take one. If someone insisted on taking a picture, he would say,
"Hide behind me. I will block you." If someone pursued me with a camera
after I asked them not to, he would talk to them and ask them to stop.

In so many ways, he was my shield.

I awoke this morning with the sun in my eyes, feeling very vulnerable. Mark was not here to draw the curtains. I got up and did the things he normally did. Fed the cats. Started the coffee. Today, I not only feel lonely—I feel unprotected.

I recall how, on those first few nights by myself after all friends and family had returned home, I felt intense fear. I am not a fearful person, but the darkness, the quietness, and the aloneness combined to make me cry out to God.

As usual, He answered me.

> *He will cover you with his feathers, and under his wings you will find refuge; his faithfulness will be your shield and rampart. You will not fear the terror of night, nor the arrow that flies by day. (Psalm 91:4–5)*

I know that even while trusting God, I am not immune to troubles and harm. But I also know that whatever happens must be allowed by God.

Yes, I have a home security system, but my true security comes from God. Sometimes in those fearful nights, I would actually say out loud, "God is my security." I tried to focus on the unlimited power of a loving, protecting Father instead of the weakness of the scared little girl I was at that moment.

I have lost the physical protection of a loving husband, but God will shelter me under His wings.

PRAYER

Lord, remind me daily that You are my true security. Let me trust You completely and find in You the comfort I need.

MEDITATION

May the LORD answer you when you are in distress; may the name of the God of Jacob protect you. (Psalm 20:1)

We have this hope as an anchor for the soul, firm and secure. (Hebrews 6:19)

FINDING HOPE IN THE DARKNESS

thoughts to remember

I think of Jesus on the cross as He breathed His last and surrendered to the will of the Father. It is because of His last breath that I will breathe the air of heaven forever.

Just Breathe

Sometimes, I miss my husband so much I can't breathe. My sobs choke me, and I gasp for each breath. I yearn to be with him, to see him again. I know that is not possible, and when we do meet in heaven, we will no longer be husband and wife. Since I have not yet broken these chains to earth, I can't stop thinking of him—his arms around me, my head on his chest.

I try to control the sobs by breathing slowly. In and out. Consciously slowing my breaths and concentrating on the arms of God around me. It is a hard truth that the arms around me now are invisible and ethereal. Still, my very breathing reminds me that God is with me.

> *Then the LORD God formed a man from the dust of the ground and breathed into his nostrils the breath of life, and the man became a living being. (Genesis 2:7)*

God's Word is filled with His breath of life. 2 Timothy 3:16 says that all Scripture is God-breathed. When we read it, we are being filled with His life-giving breath. I like to read it out loud, praying back His words to Him. It is powerful and comforting, and I know He is pleased.

Scripture relates example after example of God's breath changing lives, from Genesis, where life was created, to Job affirming that "In his hand is the life of every creature and the breath of all mankind" (Job 12:10), to Paul, who proclaims that God "gives everyone life and breath and everything else" (Acts 17:25).

I am now often very conscious of my breathing, especially after watching Mark slowly exhale his final breath in this world. Thankfully, he passed very peacefully; just as God put breath in him, He took it away slowly. Sometimes,

I think of God and purposefully inhale deeply, as if I could pull the Spirit of God into my lungs.

I admit I did not want to breathe any longer after Mark died. I wanted God to take these breaths away, just as He did for Mark. I wanted to exhale my last on this earth and inhale the sweet scent of heaven. But that was not in God's plan. Every day I wake to new breaths, but with those breaths come new challenges, new purposes, and new revelations of the love of God.

I think of Jesus on the cross as He breathed His last and surrendered to the will of the Father. It is because of His last breath that I will breathe the air of heaven forever.

When sobs choke my breath, I consider the work of Jesus who died to give me life. I will use each breath, each day He gives me, to glorify Him.

PRAYER

Lord, You have given me breath. You have given me life. Help me to live and breathe for You.

MEDITATION

Let everything that has breath praise the LORD. Praise the LORD. (Psalm 150:6)

This is what God the LORD says—the Creator of the heavens, who stretches them out, who spreads out the earth with all that springs from it, who gives breath to its people, and life to those who walk on it. (Isaiah 42:5)

thoughts to remember

FINDING HOPE IN THE DARKNESS

Fingerprints

It is startling to find evidence of Mark around the house in unexpected places. In the basement, I glanced at the rafters to find a pencil balanced there. It could only have been placed there by Mark. The find, as simple as it was, brought tears. The last person to touch that pencil was Mark. He put it there because he thought he would be back for it.

Sometimes I open a drawer and find a note in his handwriting. It could be a list of things to do around the house or someone's phone number, or even words I don't understand. But the note immediately becomes precious to me. I can't throw it away. It was from him, and I will never have another.

These objects become almost sacred to me, like some kind of relic. They were touched by my loved one who is no more. Especially moving are the cards he sent to me. I was never really much of a sentimentalist and tossed many cards. For some reason, I saved the last anniversary card he had given me. It said that the only thing he would have changed about our marriage is that he would have married me sooner. He had no idea our time together would be cut so short.

I continue to find his fingerprints everywhere. His workbench is piled with projects he had planned. His clothes were hung in the closet, ready for the next day. To-do lists, notes, discarded pens, and half-read books with markers where he stopped can derail my day.

Some items I dealt with immediately. I had Mark's brother and close friend remove his clothes from our bedroom closet. I could not bear to see everything arranged so neatly for a day that would never arrive.

I remember where we bought each picture on the wall. The scratches on the furniture speak of guests and parties. Even the paint on the walls reminds me of joint decisions and disagreements, working together to create our home. A home that is no longer ours.

This house is too big for me, but how can I leave it? It is filled with Mark's fingerprints. How can I bear the thought of someone erasing them? It is hard to stay, but harder to move.

Every time I find an unexpected treasure, I hear God whisper, "He is with me." It gives me comfort and sorrow at the same time. He is not here to leave more fingerprints.

Every night I look out my bedroom window and see the night sky, filled with twinkling stars and changing constellations. I wonder if Mark is skipping from planet to planet and playing among the stars. It makes me feel connected to him. I can see the stars; I just can't see Mark.

> *The heavens declare the glory of God; the skies proclaim the work of his hands. (Psalm 19:1)*

I can see God's handiwork. The beauty of the sky, the majesty of the earth—all are God's fingerprints. I can't miss His creativity and loving touch when I look around me. I see something new each day: a new flower, a picture of deep space. God is found in all of creation. We just need to open our eyes.

I keep my eyes open for fingerprints Mark left behind. When they are found, I treasure them all. God's fingerprints are infinite, and because Mark bore the fingerprint of his Creator, he will be treasured forever. ✳

PRAYER

Lord, help me to treasure Your fingerprints in this world. I rejoice that Mark held Your imprint, and one day, we will be reunited.

MEDITATION

The people walking in darkness have seen a great light; on those living in the land of deep darkness a light has dawned. (Isaiah 9:2)

So we fix our eyes not on what is seen, but on what is unseen, since what is seen is temporary, but what is unseen is eternal. (2 Corinthians 4:18)

FINDING HOPE IN THE DARKNESS

thoughts to remember

FINDING HOPE IN THE DARKNESS

Be Still

I hear noises in the house I never heard before. The whirring and clack of the refrigerator, the clunk of the sump pump when it rains, the loud ticking of a clock can all break the silence of the evening. These are sounds I never paid attention to before. I notice them now because there is no conversation, no human voices to fill the void.

Sometimes, I turn on the TV just for noise. The long stretches of stillness make me focus on my loss, and I need to hear human voices instead of the soft meows of the cats. I don't even pay attention to what is being said on the TV. I complete my tasks to the unfocused buzz of speech that at least makes me believe I am not the only person in the world. The noise drowns out the cacophony in my heart that reminds me my husband is gone.

The one time I can really tolerate silence is when I am reading God's Word. That is a time I need to focus on the message before me. Some people can function with constant noise in their lives. I find I can't hear God clearly when the TV or music is piercing the quiet. God tells me to quiet my soul so I can hear Him.

Sometimes there is so much distraction in my life; I can't quiet my soul even when my physical world is bathed in silence. I struggle with the dissonance of my emotions. I hear the cries of my loneliness, my impassioned pleas for mercy, the shattering of my heart. The interference of my life drowns out the whispers of God. It is a struggle to submit myself to the stillness of the presence of God. I pray the Holy Spirit leads me in quietness so that the Word of God can truly penetrate my heart.

How often do I miss what God is telling me because I am drowning out His whispers of love with shouts of my own pain? How often do I clamor to be heard when God has something to tell me? There is nothing wrong with prayers of supplication. In fact, God wants me to bring my requests before Him. But there are also times I need to simply be still and listen for His voice.

> *Be still before the LORD and wait patiently for him. (Psalm 37:7)*

God hears all my prayers—loud, soft, and even inaudible. He hears loud sobbing and heart-wrenching groans. He will answer all my prayers according to His will. I need to concentrate not on how loudly I can make my request, but on how still I can be to hear His answers.

PRAYER

Lord, help me quiet my noisy heart. Help me to hear You in the stillness and trust in Your love.

MEDITATION

A time to tear and a time to mend, a time to be silent and a time to speak. (Ecclesiastes 3:7)

It is good to wait quietly for the salvation of the LORD. (Lamentations 3:26)

thoughts to remember

FINDING HOPE IN THE DARKNESS

Playing Solitaire

There are always subtle reminders that I am now alone. A single banana sits on the counter. Mark ate one a day, so we always had a bunch. At the grocery store, I buy one piece of salmon and single-serve portions of desserts. I can no longer use "buy one, get one free" coupons because the other "one" will most likely go to waste. I am a party of one.

I play solitaire at night. No more games that need two people to play. I know I could play against a computer, but that makes me feel even more alone. There were so many activities we did as a couple that I no longer have a desire to do as a single. We often went to museums or craft shows, and I can't imagine doing those things without him. So, I play solitaire.

I know my loss does not define me. I am still a complete person. However, I cannot shake the feeling that I am a single in a couple's world, a solitaire player at a bridge game. Part of mourning my loss is adapting to my husband's absence. At this point, there are days I don't want to adapt. I want to cry over the memories of things we did together, things that I can't bring myself to do alone. I know it is okay to cry. It is just exhausting and draining, and I don't feel I can afford to be drained of anything else.

> *My eyes are dim with grief. I call to you, LORD,*
> *every day; I spread out my hands to you. (Psalm 88:9)*

I have asked, "How long will grief last?" Of course, there is no answer. It lasts as long as it lasts. It is now several months since Mark's death. I don't know how I will feel six months from now. Will the pain be less? Will I not cry every day? God only asks that I live each day at a time. I am trying, but some days are more difficult to want to live than others.

The only comfort I have is that while physically, I am alone, spiritually, I never will be. God hears my cries for mercy. God sees me distressed and grieving. God is with me through it all. God's ways are not my ways, so I must trust Him, even when I don't feel His presence or sense His comfort.

Although He was surrounded by disciples, Jesus lived a solitary life. No one could understand what He went through. No one could understand the specter of the cross looming in His future. When He needed friends the most, they denied and deserted Him. Jesus understands my solitaire games like no one else. Because He endured being utterly forsaken, I never will be.

PRAYER

Lord, be merciful to me when I am distressed. You see my grief and sorrow. You share my pain. Let me look to You for comfort.

MEDITATION

Answer me when I call to you, my righteous God. Give me relief from my distress; have mercy on me and hear my prayer. (Psalm 4:1)

And the peace of God, which transcends all understanding, will guard your hearts and your minds in Christ Jesus. (Philippians 4:7)

thoughts to remember

FINDING HOPE IN THE DARKNESS

First, Get Your Feet Wet

My widowhood does not define me, but it has changed me. I can't help but think differently and even act differently. My husband had certain roles and responsibilities that he no longer performs. He always took the lead in home repair projects or anything having to do with electricity or plumbing. When there was need for a contractor, I expected him to make contact. I felt insecure in making decisions about things of which I had no knowledge. When I had to replace the tires on my car, he was the one I went to for assistance. When the sump pump died and the basement started taking on water, he was the one who took care of it. I never thought much about his presence in my times of need. He was there all the time, and I am sad to say I took him for granted. Now that he is gone, I miss not only his presence but also his actions.

There were so many tasks he did that I never even considered—tasks that were outside of his job description. Yes, he took out the trash and maintained the yard, but he also played nurse when I had surgery on my foot. He brought home a bell for me so I could ring it when I needed him. He killed the nuclear centipedes that found their way inside the house because they would make my skin crawl. When I wanted to shop, he would go along and carry all my bags because he knew my desire for retail therapy would last longer than my aching back. He built a raised garden bed for me when my joints could no longer withstand hours of weeding on my knees. It is hard for me to think I will never be able to thank him in this life for all he did.

Now I am on my own, and I must battle my own nuclear centipedes. It is daunting and often frustrating to figure out ways of accomplishing things Mark did that I never paid attention to. One day, I wanted to hang a basket with flowers on the wall. I thought it would be an easy enough task. But first,

I could not find hangers. What would I use? A nail? A hook? Then, I could not find a hammer. How could such a simple task be so difficult? Eventually, I broke down in tears, not because I couldn't hang the basket but because Mark was not here to do it.

God is calling me into new territory. I don't know what lies ahead. To be honest, it is frightening. I trust God, but I don't necessarily trust me. I was paralyzed in hanging the basket because I thought of everything I could do wrong. I could hang it crooked. I could end up with multiple holes in the wall. I could puncture something with the nail. I only focused on what I couldn't do, not on what God could do through me.

I thought of the Israelites crossing the Jordan with the Ark of the Covenant and moving into the Promised Land. What did they feel when they saw that immense barrier? Did they think, as I did, "I can't do this. I'm doomed"? God ended up parting the river to renew and strengthen their faith, but not immediately. First, they had to get their feet wet.

> *And as soon as the priests who carry the ark of the LORD—the Lord of all the earth—set foot in the Jordan, its waters flowing downstream will be cut off and stand up in a heap. (Joshua 3:13)*

Not only did the Israelites have to cross the Jordan, but they also had to cross it when it was at flood stage. They were faced with a task they could not humanly accomplish. God could have simply parted the waters as He did at the Red Sea. But, this time, He waited for the Israelites to show their faith. The priests' feet had to get wet before the waters miraculously parted.

God is leading me to boundaries that terrify and overwhelm me. I need to perform tasks I feel I am not capable of doing. I am definitely outside of my comfort zone. Still, God has promised to be with me. In order to renew and strengthen my faith, He is asking me first to get my feet wet. I need to step out where I can't see where I am going. I need to speak out when I don't know if I will be received. In every case, I can rely on God to bring me through.

Eventually, I found an alternate way of hanging the basket. It is a reminder that God is calling me to do things I never did before, big and small, and that He will give me wisdom and patience to accomplish all that He asks.

PRAYER

Lord, You are asking me to journey in a strange land. I must do what I have never done before. Remind me, as You ask me to step out in faith, that You do not ask me to journey alone, for You are with me every step of the way.

MEDITATION

Have I not commanded you? Be strong and courageous. Do not be afraid; do not be discouraged, for the LORD your God will be with you wherever you go. (Joshua 1:9)

But blessed is the one who trusts in the LORD, whose confidence is in him. (Jeremiah 17:7)

thoughts to remember

FINDING HOPE IN THE DARKNESS

Am I so focused on my failures, on my inadequacies, that I miss the heart of God?

FINDING HOPE IN THE DARKNESS

Beautiful

As I was getting ready one day, I thought of women whose husbands called them beautiful. Some might not be considered attractive by the world's standards, but their husbands, looking through the eyes of love, saw a beauty others did not. I mourned that Mark never called me beautiful. In my presence, he had casually told other women they looked beautiful, and each time, my stomach twisted with the sound. I had figured I wasn't beautiful, so why would he ever call me that? If he didn't think I was beautiful, I didn't want him to lie, so I never brought it up.

One thing I miss dearly is how he would come home every night and call out, "I'm home, lovely wife." Often, when he couldn't see me, he would call, "Where are you, lovely wife?" He would address cards "To my lovely wife." He would even introduce me to others as his lovely wife, yet I never heard the word I wanted to hear—beautiful. I had to settle for lovely.

Mark and I sometimes had difficulty expressing our innermost thoughts and emotions to each other. We did not always speak clearly so the other could completely understand. After he passed away, I decided to look up the dictionary meaning of lovely. I was stunned when I saw that lovely actually means "exquisitely beautiful." Not just beautiful. Exquisitely beautiful.

I dissolved into tears. All those years, Mark had been telling me I was more than beautiful to him, and I couldn't hear it because I was waiting to hear "the" word. He never called another woman lovely. I completely missed his heart because I was focusing on my inadequacies. I felt unattractive, so how could he ever feel I was? What else did I miss?

Is this how I am treating God? Am I so focused on my failures, on my inadequacies, that I miss the heart of God? Again and again, He tells me He loves me, but I think, "That can't be for me. He doesn't think of me that way."

But God never gives up on us. He asks that we stop focusing on ourselves and look to Him. He desires to love us, to care for us. He loves us with an everlasting love. He wants us to trust Him, to love Him back.

> *The LORD appeared to us in the past, saying: "I have loved you with an everlasting love; I have drawn you with unfailing kindness." (Jeremiah 31:3)*

I pray I never miss God's expressions of love the way that I missed Mark's.

PRAYER

Lord, open my eyes to Your many expressions of love. When I can't feel love, Your Word reminds me that I am and always will be loved by You.

MEDITATION

But from everlasting to everlasting the LORD's love is with those who fear him, and his righteousness with their children's children. (Psalm 103:17)

He has made everything beautiful in its time. He has also set eternity in the human heart; yet no one can fathom what God has done from beginning to end. (Ecclesiastes 3:11)

thoughts to remember

FINDING HOPE IN THE DARKNESS

Laments

People often ask me how I am doing. If it is someone I am just meeting, or someone I don't know well, the answer is more than likely, "Fine." I can't drop my sack of grief on them and expect them to understand or even care. They didn't know my husband. They cannot fathom the depth of my loss.

If it is a close friend, I might tell them how I am *actually* doing, which can range from "not doing too badly" to "in a puddle on the ground." I can share my struggles with them because they have walked with me through the swamp of tears I have shed. They, too, have their own swamps to navigate. We can be honest with each other.

I love the Psalms because they always show the brutal honesty of the Psalmist. If he is joyous, he is dancing with raised arms. If he has a request, he is on his knees, pleading before the Lord. If he is grieving, he is drenching his bed with tears and fearing being pulled into his grave because of his great sorrow.

These last months, there has been little, if any, dancing in my house. Certainly, I could use kneepads because of the many times I have been upon my knees, pleading with God for mercy and compassion in my grief. It feels like most of the time, I follow in the example of the Psalmist and also have drenched my bed with tears. But God can handle my lamentations. His Word even gives me a model for my cries.

> *I cry aloud to the LORD; I lift up my voice to the LORD for mercy. I pour out before him my complaint; before him I tell my trouble. When my spirit grows faint within me, it is you who watch over my way. In the path where I walk people have hidden a snare for me. Look and see, there is no one at my right hand; no one is concerned for me. I have no refuge; no one cares for my life. I cry to you, LORD; I say, "You are my refuge, my portion in the land of the living." (Psalm 142:1–5)*

As so frequently happens, these words from the Psalms perfectly express how I am feeling. I cry before God. I tell him how miserable and sorrowful and depressed I am. I feel faint with grief, and people don't always make it better with their "encouraging" words (encouraging like Job's friends). I once had a husband, and I was his priority. I could depend on him to support and protect me. Now, I have no one for whom I am Number One. There are always others who will come first. Except, of course, with God. He watches over my way. He is my refuge. God has not left me alone in the land of the living.

Life continues to be confusing and sorrowful. I struggle with loneliness and longing every day, and especially every night. It is comforting to be able to take these cares to someone who not only understands but has given me the words to express my feelings even more completely. Reading the Psalms invites brutal honesty in my conversations with God. I know that God not only tolerates my laments; He desires my expression of them. Like the Psalmist, complete honesty before God will only draw me closer to Him and give me a better understanding of His love and concern.

PRAYER

Lord, let me always be completely, brutally honest with You concerning my emotions and fears. Help me to understand that You desire to hear me, whether I am praising You or complaining to You.

MEDITATION

I am worn out from my groaning. All night long I flood my bed with weeping and drench my couch with tears. (Psalm 6:6)

Why, my soul, are you downcast? Why so disturbed within me? Put your hope in God, for I will yet praise him, my Savior and my God. (Psalm 42:5)

thoughts to remember

FINDING HOPE IN THE DARKNESS

Lord, I Am Willing

Some days, I hate to get out of bed. What's the point? My husband is gone, along with my hopes and dreams for the future. If it wasn't for the tenacious meowing of the cats to get up and feed them, I would pull the blankets over my head and stay there.

Recently, it hasn't been just the cats getting me out of bed. I feel an urging and hear a voice deep within me, saying, "Get up. I have work for you." The Spirit of God is as persistent as the brightening daylight. As I travel in my grief journey, I hear Him more often. Perhaps I am listening more intently. But I am more and more aware that He has a job for me to do. Am I willing to do it?

It would be easy to ignore the world, both physical and spiritual, right now. No one would think less of me. I have gone through one of the most painful, most stressful experiences a person can endure—the loss of a spouse. If, on some days, I wanted to spend the day crying in a darkened room, that would be understandable. Some days I do, but not most days. I know God left me here on earth for a purpose. I am not entirely sure what that purpose is, but I know it exists.

> *"For I know the plans I have for you,"*
> *declares the LORD, "plans to prosper you and not to harm you,*
> *plans to give you hope and a future." (Jeremiah 29:11)*

Jeremiah 29:11 was one of my husband's and my favorite verses. After he died, I felt like the verse was a cruel joke. How could I prosper without Mark? How could his death not harm me? What kind of hope and future would I have now? But, as I told myself so often, the truth of God's Word does not depend on my emotions. Whether I believe it or not, God has a plan.

Today, God's plan for me is simply living. It is important to Him that I take care of my health, both physically and mentally. Slowly, He is revealing the tasks He has for me. If I trust Him, He will make them the desire of my heart. I am writing more. I am leading a women's Bible study. I am meeting with other widows who have a spiritual hunger to know why I believe what I do. God is giving me opportunities, and as I accept each one, He will give me more.

It is not easy to accept some of these tasks. I have a tendency to get stuck on thinking of my failures and inadequacies. Yet, I know if God gives me something to do, He will help me do it. I just have to be willing to try.

PRAYER

Lord, open my eyes to opportunities to serve You. Help me when I feel weak or inadequate. Show me hope and encourage me that You have my future under control.

MEDITATION

Commit to the LORD whatever you do, and he will establish your plans.
(Proverbs 16:3)

And the God of all grace, who called you to his eternal glory in Christ, after you have suffered a little while, will himself restore you and make you strong, firm and steadfast.
(1 Peter 5:10)

thoughts to remember

FINDING HOPE IN THE DARKNESS

Prey

In the early days of my grief, I had much fear. I feared being alone in the house at night. I feared I would not be able to keep up with the house and yard. I feared being single for the rest of my life. My fears multiplied daily.

Some of my fears were based in reality. I needed to be cognizant of my cash flow because I was now operating on one fixed income. I needed help with the house and yard because I was incapable of doing all that had to be done. Other fears were strictly imagined. Would I be alone for the rest of my life? Possibly. But fearing the future would not change it, and I do not know what God has planned for the rest of my life.

I could not let fear paralyze me. I needed to take action to alleviate as many fears as I could. I had a home security system installed. I hired a lawn service. For the fears I couldn't control, I had to learn to cast my destiny into the waiting arms of God.

Easier said than done.

It was easy for me to become overwhelmed with fear. I felt as though I was wounded prey to these predatory thoughts. In fact, God's Word confirmed I actually **was** being hunted:

> *Be alert and of sober mind. Your enemy the devil prowls around like a roaring lion looking for someone to devour. (1 Peter 5:8)*

The enemy of my soul would like nothing more than for me to be consumed by sorrow, to take my eyes off the Shepherd who leads me. He pounces on my grieving heart at every opportunity, tearing and ripping at my faith. He is ruthless and cruel in his unrelenting attacks in areas where I am most vulnerable.

I will not be prey to this beast.

While I know Jesus is my Shepherd who protects me, I must also take action to obey God's Word. God's Word tells me to be "alert and of sober mind." I can't become complacent in my grief. I must continuously seek God's direction to keep moving forward. I need to acknowledge the attacks of the enemy and call in reinforcement prayer from friends if necessary.

I must also remain clearheaded. Grief clouds my thinking, and I am more susceptible to the lies of the devil. I need to constantly test my thoughts to be sure they align with God's Word. Any thoughts of self-harm or rejection or failure do not originate from God.

I pray for God's protection from roaring lions. One day, the lion will be caged and my freedom will be eternal.

PRAYER

Lord, You are my Protector, my Shepherd who keeps me safe. Do not let me stray from Your loving arms.

MEDITATION

Do not withhold your mercy from me, LORD; may your love and faithfulness always protect me. (Psalm 40:11)

But the Lord is faithful, and he will strengthen you and protect you from the evil one. (2 Thessalonians 3:3)

thoughts to remember

FINDING HOPE IN THE DARKNESS

Tears In A Bottle

I really have not been much of a crier in my adult life. I cried deeply when my parents died and at the deaths of other loved ones. I have had tears in my eyes at emotionally charged movies and events. In actuality, Mark cried more than I did. I held myself in check, mostly from years of a high-stress job where tears were considered a sign of weakness. I had to maintain control. Sometimes, other women would tell me to "let it all out" while listing the benefits of a good cry. But I saw only the awkwardness of public tears and thought of the swollen eyes and puffy face that would inevitably follow.

When Mark was taken to the hospital, I didn't cry. I knew his situation was grave, but I thought we would get through the difficult times together, and with rehab, he would be okay. I called my friends to tell them what was going on, and although my voice was shaky, I don't remember crying. This was a difficult time that needed to be addressed, and I was simply calling for back-up. It was not until the doctor told me he would never speak, walk, or even feed himself again that my guard dissolved into tears.

I never understood how deeply a person could feel sorrow. I loved my parents greatly and certainly mourned their passing. I even cried over the deaths of my cats because they were part of my family. I had lost friends and family, and each time, I cried. It wasn't that I couldn't cry. I just chose the appropriate time and place. I controlled tears. They did not control me.

But there I was, in a hospital, being told my husband—if he survived— would never be the same. Then came the news of the brain bleed and that the left side of his brain was dead. Then, the final pronouncement. He was brain-dead.

I sat by his side, waiting for his final breath. Friends surrounded me, but I saw only him, his head scarred from the surgery to relieve pressure on his brain, his face serene and quiet. How handsome he looked as I gently stroked his soft beard. I didn't want him to leave me. Yet, he heard the call of God.

I am not sure I ever stopped crying from the initial diagnosis. I think I was in shock. All I can remember are tears, more tears than I had cried in my lifetime. Tears ran down my face and wet my clothes. As Mark lay in the casket, tears dropped into his beard and shirt. Tears in what little food I could eat. Unstoppable, copious tears.

When finally home alone, the tears ripped my soul. I wailed in pain. I doubted my sanity. I cried until I was exhausted, and then I cried more. Did God see me? Did He care?

> *Record my misery; list my tears on your scroll—are they not in your record? (Psalm 56:8)*

Some translations say that God keeps our tears in a bottle. The point is God not only knows of our tears, but He also treasures them. They are holy tears.

My stoic reserve concerning crying was broken. Whenever I think of Mark, I cry. I can no longer control it. I cried while passing a fast food restaurant we frequented when going on vacation. I cried walking through the men's department of a store. I cried when I looked into my backyard and saw the beauty of all he had accomplished. I cried with loss while thinking of the things we would never share again.

Tears are part of mourning. I cannot and should not try to stop them. I sometimes try to rearrange them so they occur in a less public place. They will still come.

Jesus was the perfect man, yet the Bible records times when Jesus cried. God not only understands the depths of our emotions, but He also experienced them.

I still cry often. I am sure God is tracking at least my second jug of tears. There is comfort in knowing God has seen and treasured each and every tear. He has not forgotten me in my sorrow. We cry together, and one day, we will rejoice together as my captured tears will be only memories.

PRAYER

Lord, help me to understand that the tears I cry are sacred. They are memories of one I loved deeply and miss greatly. I know Your tears are mingled with mine.

MEDITATION

Those who sow with tears will reap with songs of joy. (Psalm 126:5)

"Where have you laid him?" he asked. "Come and see, Lord," they replied. Jesus wept. (John 11:34–35)

thoughts to remember

FINDING HOPE IN THE DARKNESS

FINDING HOPE IN THE DARKNESS

Trust

Trust is so tenuous. We can trust God for something momentous like physical healing and then falter over something simple like passing a test. In some ways, it is easier to trust for a miracle than it is for day-to-day life.

We feel we are in control. We have it covered. We need God for the big decisions, but we can handle the small stuff. We can work and earn money to pay our bills. We can maintain our relationships with a smile. We can provide for ourselves.

The fact is, we control nothing. God is the giver and sustainer of life. He is our provider. Without Him, we can do nothing. With Him, all things are possible.

When tragedy strikes, we are stunned. How could God let this happen? Was He distracted? Does He not care?

> *See, I have engraved you on the palms of my hands; your walls are ever before me. (Isaiah 49:16)*

The fact is, even in tragedy, in suffering, in the deepest grief, God is in control. God knew Mark's appointed time, and nothing could change that. God knows my condition, my future, and my desires, and no amount of my fretting will impact God's design, for His design is for my good and His glory.

I continue to pray because I am obedient to God's command. Will it change anything? I don't know. I do know it changes my perspective from being centered on me to being centered on God. I pray because I know God is able. Whether or not He is willing is up to Him.

There is comfort in knowing I am not in control. Life is too great a risk. I cannot trust myself to always act in my best interests. My humanity too often gets in the way, and I seek comfort instead of growth or happiness instead of holiness. God has promised to give us direction if we ask for it. He has engraved us on the palms of His hands and will never forget us.

That I can trust in. ❊

PRAYER

Lord, help me to understand that because You are in control of my life, I do not need to fear what the future may hold. You hold me in the palm of Your hand, next to Your heart, and will never let me go.

MEDITATION

I keep my eyes always on the LORD. With him at my right hand, I will not be shaken. (Psalm 16:8)

He will not let your foot slip—he who watches over you will not slumber; indeed, he who watches over Israel will neither slumber nor sleep. (Psalm 121:3-4)

thoughts to remember

FINDING HOPE IN THE DARKNESS

What I Need

Wild, uncontrollable thoughts ran through my mind after Mark passed away. I couldn't comprehend his death, but I knew my life had changed dramatically. I knew I had lost a husband, but it took me some time to realize how much more I had lost.

I began to think of all the things Mark once did, things I would need help doing. For some reason, taking care of the yard was a daunting and terrifying task. I had never mowed grass before. I had weeded flowerbeds, and I had an herb garden, but the majority of the yard work had been his. There were multiple flowerbeds, a vegetable garden, a seemingly vast array of daylilies (his favorite), trees, and shrubs—the list went on and on. How could I care for them the way Mark did?

I thought of household chores. He was on cat litter box duty and scooped and changed the litter. Because of the weight of the litter for two cat boxes, I was skeptical I could even perform this task with my severely arthritic back.

There was also the reality of the house. We were in the middle of remodeling the kitchen and family room. A small wall had been removed, and consequently, holes were present in the floor and walls. Painting was only half-finished. Furniture had been moved and draped with drop cloths. Pictures were off the walls. It was a construction zone. The thought of putting it back together without Mark was overwhelming.

The list went on and on. Who would fix the leaky bathroom faucet? Who would install the laundry room light? Who would repair the doorbell? Who would help me live life?

My needs overwhelmed and depressed me. Whenever I thought of what I needed, my anxiety rose. I cried. I couldn't sleep. As anxiety coupled with the immense sorrow over the loss of my husband, I became a complete mess.

Thankfully, my friends stepped in to help me. They assured me I could find a lawn service to mow the lawn, and a friend came over almost weekly to help with the rest of the yard work. She even planted tomatoes in the vegetable garden. It may not have been the way Mark did it, but, as she reminded me, the yard was under new management.

For some household chores, an alternate completion method was needed. I found a lightweight cat litter I could actually lift. I used cleaning supplies that made the task easier. I found a reliable handyman for the jobs I was not comfortable completing (anything electrical or plumbing related).

My friends and family united to help me put the kitchen and family room back into working order. They completed painting, patched walls, and moved furniture. Although I still have a hole in the floor, I can live with that being a future repair.

My needs were stated and met. For jobs still needing completion, I have promises of help. But there is one need no one can assist with. In fact, even when Mark was alive, he could not help me with it.

The one need that every individual has is the need for Jesus Christ.

> *What is more, I consider everything a loss because of the surpassing worth of knowing Christ Jesus my Lord, for whose sake I have lost all things. I consider them garbage, that I may gain Christ. (Philippians 3:8)*

Obviously, there is worth in relationships and purpose in life. God created marriage and called it good. But all these things pale in comparison to the knowledge of Christ.

Physical needs were taken care of, and friends tried hard to meet what emotional needs they could. No one could fill the void of a missing husband, nor did they try. They helped me work through my loss as best they could. But, with them or alone, I still feel the pull of eternity; I feel the space in my soul that only God can fill.

My greatest need has been—and will always be—God. Jesus Christ in my life is the only answer to this need.

PRAYER

Lord, I am humbled by knowing that You, the Creator and Sustainer of all life, knows my needs. You meet me daily with mercy and grace, and I thank You for allowing me to know You.

MEDITATION

For God so loved the world that he gave his one and only Son, that whoever believes in him shall not perish but have eternal life. (John 3:16)

So that Christ may dwell in your hearts through faith. And I pray that you, being rooted and established in love, may have power, together with all the Lord's holy people, to grasp how wide and long and high and deep is the love of Christ, and to know this love that surpasses knowledge—that you may be filled to the measure of all the fullness of God. (Ephesians 3:17–19)

thoughts to remember

FINDING HOPE IN THE DARKNESS

> *I think of Jesus holding my hands as I sob. He gently puts a hand on my shoulder. When I look into His eyes, there are tears there.*

FINDING HOPE IN THE DARKNESS

Weep With Me

My husband was the social half of our marriage. He could talk to anyone at any time. It sometimes even caused friction between us when we were out to dinner and he spent his evening talking to the strangers at the table next to us instead of to his wife. It was really just a difference in personality. Now that I am alone, I can't rely on him for social interactions. I have my friends, but to avoid burning them out, I am trying to expand my social circle. I now talk to people I would have never talked to before. However, this is not without its challenges.

While my friends are very familiar with the quirks in my personality, other people have no idea who I really am. I find my jokes falling flat. Or, even worse, I find I can be completely misunderstood. At this point in my journey, I can't find a balance between reaching out to others or punching them in the face with my grief. Part of the difficulty is my emotions, which are unpredictable and close to the surface. I suppose I can be a little frightening at times for those who don't know me.

All I am trying to do is connect with another person. When Mark was unplugged from my life, I lost power. The spark was gone. I am slowly trying to regain my sociability, my desire to be with others.

Yet, I know it will never be the same. I will always feel his absence, and that loss affects all I do. When I meet new people, the conversation inevitably turns to loss and grief and all that is associated with the word "widow."

What do I really want from people? To be honest, I want them to understand, even just a little, the depth of my pain. I don't want advice; I don't want pity. There are no words to alleviate my grief. But I do want them to reach out to me. To listen to me. To weep with me.

I realize that is something difficult for close friends to do; I can't expect it from new acquaintances.

> *Each heart knows its own bitterness, and no one else can share its joy.*
> *(Proverbs 14:10)*

I find myself thinking of Jesus when I cry. The pain and loneliness still threaten to swallow my evenings. I think of Jesus holding my hands as I sob. He gently puts a hand on my shoulder. When I look into His eyes, there are tears there.

These are such hard truths to understand. I am alone, but God is with me always. My dreams are shattered, but God says He has a plan for my life. I feel unloved, but He loves me with an everlasting love. I struggle to get past my emotions and to God's truth.

Whether my friends understand my pain or not, whether I will meet someone who can relate to what I am experiencing or not, the truth never changes.

When I weep, Jesus weeps with me.

PRAYER

Lord, I know You feel my pain and loneliness. Only You can truly understand what I am going through. Help me to get past my emotions so that I may live in Your truth.

MEDITATION

May your unfailing love be my comfort, according to your promise to your servant.
(Psalm 119:76)

Before I formed you in the womb I knew you, before you were born I set you apart.
(Jeremiah 1:5)

FINDING HOPE IN THE DARKNESS

thoughts to remember

FINDING HOPE IN THE DARKNESS

Griefquakes

Just when I begin to feel better, a griefquake hits. I had gotten to the point of not crying as deeply as before. I cried in memory, and I cried in loneliness, but I was no longer crying in despair. The change was probably a result of time, counseling, and finding distractions. But then, sorting through the mountains of paperwork that just were parked on my desk and never moved, the griefquake hit, and I was swept away in emotion. I miss everything about Mark, both the good and the bad.

The good was very, very good. We shared the same personality in many ways. Our senses of humor, our likes and dislikes. We were matched. The bad was very, very bad. At times, he shut me out completely, unable to separate his difficult past from the present with me. I sometimes felt lonely in marriage, but I had no idea of the unrelenting depth of loneliness in death.

My heart aches with memories of the times I was less than kind to him, or demanding, or just plain mean. I begged God to tell him I am sorry, and that I truly, truly loved him. I know that now, in heaven, Mark knows perfect love and perfect forgiveness, and I know he understands. But I am still here. I cry over my loss and my sin until I am choked with tears. I know he forgives me. But can I ever forgive myself?

Over and over, I remind myself of who I am in Christ. I am forgiven. I am redeemed. But I am also a living woman who struggles with loss and loneliness, guilt and pain.

I cry to God. He is the only one who will hear me 24/7 and receive me with compassion and understanding. I know that in this world, I will continue to sin, and He will continue to forgive me. He is ready for my griefquakes and will embrace me with open arms.

> *Because of the LORD's great love we are not consumed, for his compassions never fail. They are new every morning; great is your faithfulness. (Lamentations 3:22–23)*

I might not ever be able to forgive myself fully. I hope I will. But I know that God already does. In my heart, I believe Mark does as well. When the grief comes in overwhelming flows, I have nothing on earth to cling to. But I have everything in heaven to bring me through.

PRAYER

Lord, bring me through the griefquakes that occur regularly. Embrace my aching heart, and remind me I am loved and forgiven by You. In the morning, let me focus on You so that I may cling to You through every emotion of the day.

MEDITATION

But God demonstrates his own love for us in this: While we were still sinners, Christ died for us. (Romans 5:8)

I have been crucified with Christ and I no longer live, but Christ lives in me. The life I now live in the body, I live by faith in the Son of God, who loved me and gave himself for me. (Galatians 2:20)

thoughts to remember

FINDING HOPE IN THE DARKNESS

Impressions

It has been almost seven months since I lost my husband. I no longer wear my wedding rings. This is a personal choice for each widow. For me, they symbolized a marriage covenant that was pledged until death did us part. Death parted us, so the marriage is no more. I wore those rings for almost thirty-five years with love and fidelity. Now, as I look at my hand, I can see the imprint of rings on my finger.

My life will never be the same now that Mark is gone, but I am thankful for the imprint his life had on mine. He made me laugh more than any other human had, or ever will again. In his often child-like nature, he brought out the child in me, and we danced in the aisles of grocery stores and skipped in the beauty of nature. Yet there were times I was amazed at the wise insights he had into Scripture. As we stretched each other, we helped shape each other's personality.

Most importantly, we were sold out for God. God knew the time of Mark's homegoing, and in the last months of his life, I had noticed his deepening relationship with God. His worship was more personal, his love more intense. I think of him now, realizing the culmination of his search for God, and it brings me comfort.

If only the impression God has left on my life were as evident as the imprint of the rings on my finger! God has drawn me to Him, intensifying my love in every way. My worship is fuller, somehow richer. There are no boundaries now to my praise. The world has fallen away. God meets me when I pray.

My prayer is that I grow ever closer to Jesus. I want to have a deepening impression of Him on my life daily. I want to have a constant reminder that He is with me.

> *And we all, who with unveiled faces contemplate the Lord's glory, are*
> *being transformed into his image with ever-increasing glory, which comes*
> *from the Lord, who is the Spirit. (2 Corinthians 3:18)*

We wear jewelry to show our allegiance to the Lord. There are crosses on necklaces and earrings. Too often, they are worn as decoration and not as symbols of an inner relationship. I have a cross on a bracelet to remind me that God is always with me. It is not a symbol for the world to see—it is a personal declaration of faith from me to God.

Although I don't wear a wedding ring, my finger is adorned with a different reminder. I took the birthstone from a ring I gave Mark, the diamonds from a ring he gave me, and blended the gold from both to make the memorial ring I now wear. It is a reminder that although Mark is no longer with me, he will impact my life forever.

My prayer is that my heart becomes a memorial to God. I don't need an external reminder of His love, although I do find it reassuring. More than anything, I want His influence to make an eternal impression on my heart and soul. I want His likeness in me to grow, and someday, I will be perfectly like Him.

PRAYER

Lord, make a deeper impression on my life. Transform me into the image of Jesus Christ, and let me be a witness to the world of His love and forgiveness.

MEDITATION

Do not conform to the pattern of this world, but be transformed by the renewing of your mind. Then you will be able to test and approve what God's will is—his good, pleasing and perfect will. (Romans 12:2)

Who, by the power that enables him to bring everything under his control, will transform our lowly bodies so that they will be like his glorious body. (Philippians 3:21)

thoughts to remember

FINDING HOPE IN THE DARKNESS

Handling It

There is a popular saying that God will not give me more than I can handle. Totally untrue. God will often give me more than I can handle, but it will never be more than what He can handle.

I have attended an exercise class on most weekdays for many months. In the beginning, I took it easy. I didn't know how much my body could tolerate, so I didn't try adding the extra bounces or harder punches the instructor suggested. In fact, even the beginner class made me a little out of breath and red in the face. But as time went on, I found I could do more. I needed to advance to a more strenuous class. Then, even in the harder class, I needed to add the more difficult movements to be sure I was getting a good workout. If I would have started in the advanced class, I'm not sure I would have returned. But I worked my way up to it and found that the more work I put into it, the more progress I made.

God often gives me small trials to build my faith. These are the trials where I feel Him holding my hand and guiding me in the direction I should go. I am able to look back and see God's providence through my circumstances. My faith is built by His expressions of love and provision. Then, there are other times when grief and sorrow, loss and pain threaten to overwhelm me completely. Times when I can't imagine surviving the day, not to speak of the rest of my life. These are the times God allows to be absolutely more than I can handle. These are the times God says, "I will sustain you."

Sustain me, my God, according to your promise, and I will live; do not let my hopes be dashed. (Psalm 119:116)

Every day brings a new wave of grief and fear. Yet, each day also brings a new awareness of God's presence: God weeping with me, or God promising to never leave my side. I cannot see the future, but God promises to be there. I cannot see bearing this heavy burden forever, but God promises to carry me. I am drowning in sorrow, but God promises to rescue me.

God does not want me to struggle on my own, to grit my teeth, hike up my faith-pants, and forge ahead on my own power. He tells me from where I should draw that power, and it is not from within me. It is from Him.

I do not listen to the myth that I should be able to handle anything God gives me. Instead, I believe His truth, that He is the one who will sustain me and handle whatever comes my way.

PRAYER

Lord, open my eyes to Your life-sustaining power. With You carrying me, I can accomplish Your will.

MEDITATION

In the same way, the Spirit helps us in our weakness. We do not know what we ought to pray for, but the Spirit himself intercedes for us through wordless groans. (Romans 8:26)

But he said to me, "My grace is sufficient for you, for my power is made perfect in weakness." (2 Corinthians 12:9)

FINDING HOPE IN THE DARKNESS

thoughts to remember

FINDING HOPE IN THE DARKNESS

I Don't Want To Be Alone

The house is quiet. It is dark outside. I feel the tears in the corners of my eyes threatening to cascade down my cheeks. My heart is heavy with sadness, with loneliness. Even though I know God is with me, even though I have friends who love me, I still am mired in aloneness. I don't want to be alone.

There is a conflict raging in me right now. Mark is gone. I will only see him in eternity. I am still here. I don't want to be alone. I want to give and receive love, to share in the intimacies of marriage as God designed. I want to share my thoughts, hopes, fears, and even insecurities with another. I ache with aloneness. And yet, this desire also brings guilt because I am, in effect, wishing for a man to replace Mark. In my heart, I know that is not the case. I can never replace Mark; I can never erase almost thirty-five years of marriage and forget the part of me that was so untimely ripped from me. But my heart is not so sure.

I don't want to be alone.

For a long time, I would not even entertain the thought of dating again. I wanted to grow old with Mark, not start old with someone else. But the loneliness is changing to longing.

> *May he give you the desire of your heart and make all your plans*
> *succeed. (Psalm 20:4)*

What is the desire of my heart?

My thoughts are sometimes guilt-ridden and confusing. I don't think I could even identify what I truly desire. I do know this: I want what God wants for me. I will not be Abraham/Sarah who pushed their will, their way, in their time. I know what I think I want, but is that truly the best for me? In the long run, will it satisfy my desires?

I can be assured that God knows me better than I know myself. I can give Him my list of requests, but ultimately, God is the only one who can be trusted to give me not only what I desire, but also what is best for me and what will glorify Him.

My flesh cannot be trusted. It will seek to satisfy carnal desires in a way that is potentially harmful to me and dishonoring to God. My emotions cannot be trusted. They will lie and distort the truth of God's Word. My mind cannot be trusted. I can try to reason why I want what I want and how I will get it, but I do not have the mind of God and will never understand His mysterious ways. I can only trust the Word of God to shape my reality and keep me focused on living for Christ.

I don't have to worry about my desires. God knows what they are. If I allow Him, He will place them in my heart. I don't have to fear my aloneness. God understands I don't want to be alone.

PRAYER

Father, You have promised to give me the desires of my heart. Place these in me now, for my good and Your glory. Remind me, when the loneliness threatens to overtake me, that I am never truly alone, for You are always with me.

MEDITATION

So do not fear, for I am with you; do not be dismayed, for I am your God. I will strengthen you and help you; I will uphold you with my righteous right hand. (Isaiah 41:10)

"For my thoughts are not your thoughts, neither are your ways my ways," declares the LORD. "As the heavens are higher than the earth, so are my ways higher than your ways and my thoughts than your thoughts." (Isaiah 55:8–9)

thoughts to remember

> *God not only has my future in His hands, but He also has my best in His heart.*

FINDING HOPE IN THE DARKNESS

The Plunge

When I was a child, I lived next door to neighbors who had an inground pool. A chain-link fence surrounded it, but the gate was never locked, and I could jump in whenever I wanted. The problem was, although I loved being in the water and paddling around in the shallow end, I never learned to swim.

I often looked on with envy as my friends effortlessly dove into the clear, blue water and emerged smiling from its depths. They smoothly glided from one end of the pool to the other while I was confined to the shallows. Sometimes I would hold my nose and jump in, but I popped up sputtering and could only dog-paddle my way to the closest edge to climb out. Still, I loved the feeling of cool water on a hot day.

One morning I arrived at the pool before any of my friends. I didn't hesitate to let myself in the gate. Excitedly, I ran along the pool's edge to the shallow end. But there must have been a puddle because I slipped and fell into the deep water.

As I sank, I was totally disoriented. I didn't know which way was up. Everything was blue and hazy, and my head hurt where I must have hit it on the pool's edge. I kicked, but I just hit concrete. I kicked again, but I had no sense of direction and could not locate the surface. As my lungs started to burn, I was filled with panic. Which way was up? Was anyone there to save me?

I heard a gentle whisper to my heart: "Just relax." I had been struggling so hard to find my way up, and this seemed counterintuitive. "Relax." I stopped struggling and went limp. To my surprise, when I did, I floated to the top. I raised my head out of the water and climbed out, shaking and panting. I knew I could have died.

I think of that incident often as the struggles of life threaten to drown me. I remember the panic of being submerged, of not knowing which direction to go, of desperately trying to kick my way out. But I also remember the peace I felt when I finally relaxed. At the time, I didn't stop to analyze this choice, but I knew it was what I needed to do to be saved. My own efforts would have killed me; the voice of God saved me.

I never doubted it was God who told me to relax. As a child, I never questioned the existence of God or His role in my life. It wasn't until I was an adult that disbelief invaded my thinking.

When my husband died, I struggled. I kicked. I could not see my way out of the deep, overwhelming waters of grief. But in my heart, I once again heard a voice.

> *Be still, and know that I am God. (Psalm 46:10)*

Be still. Just relax. How can I do this when my world is crumbling around me? When I am drowning in grief? "Cease striving," the Lord says. The battle is His.

God not only has my future in His hands, but He also has my best in His heart. He is teaching me to swim in the waters of grief and sorrow. It may not be the effortless glide I once envied, but He has plunged me into the deep end and is protecting me there.

God is ready and willing to give me peace in deep water.

PRAYER

Lord, only You can uphold me in these deep waters by Your grace and care. I trust You as I still my heart and listen for Your love.

MEDITATION

Yes, my soul, find rest in God; my hope comes from him. (Psalm 62:5)

You will keep in perfect peace those whose minds are steadfast, because they trust in you. (Isaiah 26:3)

FINDING HOPE IN THE DARKNESS

thoughts to remember

FINDING HOPE IN THE DARKNESS

Mercy

Early in my grief, I completely lost any rational thought processes. I couldn't concentrate. Normal activities seemed useless. My appetite disappeared, and even keeping the house free of clutter and my clothes washed took tremendous effort. Grief absorbed me. I no longer felt like a person. I moved through life as a vessel of pain.

There was only one prayer I could offer to God. I cried for mercy. Over and over, with large tears washing my face, I begged and wailed for mercy. The pain was too great. I wanted release from the constant shredding of my heart, the continuous reminders of what I had lost. Mercy. I didn't want to live anymore. I wanted God to take me as well so I wouldn't have to feel any more of this pounding grief. I could barely sleep, and exhaustion made every emotion sharper. Mercy. I wanted to be numb. I wanted to just stop feeling, stop living. I wanted mercy.

God, in His mercy, did not answer these prayers. Instead, He gently told me that I couldn't sidestep grief. He took my hand and began my journey with me.

> *Out of the depths I cry to you, LORD; Lord, hear my voice. Let your ears be attentive to my cry for mercy. (Psalm 130:1–2)*

We talk about how we show mercy to animals when we remove them from pain by euthanizing them. I thought it would be a mercy if God took me out of my pain. But I am not an animal. I am a child of God, living in a sinful world filled with pain and death. Jesus, the Man of Sorrows, knows our pain. He does not take it lightly. Only God knows the reasons for our intense suffering and the loss we experience in this life. We can be assured it is not out of cruelty. God expresses His love for us on every page of His Word. Sometimes He chastens us, sometimes He draws us closer to Him, and sometimes we will simply never know why. In each case, God will meet us in our suffering.

It is difficult not to live in my emotions, but that is exactly what I must do. When I awoke this morning, I imagined Jesus waiting for me downstairs, sitting in a chair in the corner of my family room, listening for my greeting. While no one else on earth may desire my company, Jesus eagerly waits for me to enter His presence. When I meet Him there, He shows me mercy. He shows me He will be there without fail every single day of my life. He shows me I am loved unconditionally. He holds me while I am wailing in pain, even though I cannot feel Him. He reminds me of His sweet mercy shown to me on the cross.

God shows me mercy in my pain by meeting me in it. It is a matter of trust, not emotion.

Sometimes my emotions become just too strong, and I cry for mercy again. He does not turn from me when my trust falters. He holds me tighter. Someday He will tell me, face to face, all the mercies I have actually received. In the meantime, I rest in His merciful arms.

PRAYER

Lord, Your infinite, unfailing mercy envelops me every day. Thank You for never turning me away.

MEDITATION

Have mercy on me, LORD, for I am faint; heal me, LORD, for my bones are in agony. (Psalm 6:2)

Let us then approach God's throne of grace with confidence, so that we may receive mercy and find grace to help us in our time of need. (Hebrews 4:16)

FINDING HOPE IN THE DARKNESS

thoughts to remember

FINDING HOPE IN THE DARKNESS

The Mask

Sometimes I feel as though I wear a mask. Around people, I am the Widow Who Is Well, smiling and getting on with life despite adversity. I speak of how God has met me in my grief. I smile and laugh. It is not really a lie because, at times, I do feel I have risen above my grief. It is still swirling beneath me, but it does not threaten to pull me under. I can worship God with joy. I share laughter with friends. But inevitably, the darkness comes, and I am then the Widow Consumed with Grief. Like a predator, grief stalks me in the dark, quiet night and tears at my heart with sharp, deadly teeth. I feel bleeding and wounded, left for dead.

Then, the next day, it starts again.

For a time, I can find respite from the grief. There are those who truly ease my sorrow. But it is not fair to them, and it is not their responsibility to alleviate my grief. For that, I can only turn to God.

It is exhausting to live with these masks. Yet I feel people could not tolerate being with Widow Consumed with Grief all the time. It would be exhausting for them as well. I try not to wear masks around those closest to me, but life is never easy for anyone, and the thought of my additional burden on those I love makes me reach for a mask to protect them from my torment. I don't know what is acceptable behavior, and at times, my emotions wrestle any control from me. I am confused and sorrowful. I sleep but wake often, remembering what I have lost, grieving again.

The constant in-and-out of grief is draining, but I know that is how it will be for the rest of my life. I will continually lean in and out of grief—maybe just not so far in and so far out.

> *My frame was not hidden from you when I was made in the secret place,*
> *when I was woven together in the depths of the earth. Your eyes saw my*
> *unformed body; all the days ordained for me were written in your book*
> *before one of them came to be. (Psalm 139:15–16)*

I know I don't need masks with God. He knows my heart. He knows me better than I know myself. He is not intimidated or confused by my emotions. One day, the masks will fall completely, but I think that day will be when I see my Creator face to face.

PRAYER

Lord, never let me wear a mask before You. I offer You my heart and my soul, and I know You see me as I am and who I will one day be.

MEDITATION

Are not two sparrows sold for a penny? Yet not one of them will fall to the ground outside your Father's care. And even the very hairs of your head are all numbered. So don't be afraid; you are worth more than many sparrows. (Matthew 10:29-31)

From his dwelling place he watches all who live on earth—he who forms the hearts of all, who considers everything they do. (Psalm 33:14-15)

thoughts to remember

FINDING HOPE IN THE DARKNESS

Plans

Mark and I had many plans for the future. When he passed away, we were in the middle of remodeling our kitchen/family room. He was very handy around the house and had planned to do much of the work himself. I was left with half-painted walls, patching to complete, and a hole in the floor. The chaos of my home echoed the chaos of my soul when I suddenly was left a widow.

We were also planning for early retirement. We had strived all our lives to provide for a comfortable future, and God had blessed us in many ways to make this quest possible. The dream was right before us. We had about one year left before retirement. We were going to buy an RV and travel across the county, stopping to see the majestic beauty of God's creation and the historical richness of our country. We eagerly researched RV's and shopped for the features we wanted. Thankfully, we delayed actually purchasing one and had plans to do it next year.

None of our plans will ever be realized.

> *In their hearts humans plan their course, but the LORD establishes their steps. (Proverbs 16:9)*

There was nothing wrong with our making plans. God wants us to plan for the future, to use the resources and talents He has given us for our enjoyment as well as His glory. God wants His children to be happy, and we were very happy making our plans.

But ultimately, God is God, and we cannot fathom the depth of His plans for our future. We were concentrating on our happiness. We were looking forward to comfort and togetherness and a life free from stress. God, in His inscrutable ways, had other plans.

Mark died suddenly, and the shock and disbelief of his death rocked the core of my world. I not only lost my plans; I felt I had lost my entire future. I struggled not to be plunged into despair and clung to any word of hope.

I could not see a future, but God could. God was with me in those early days of grief, even when I doubted Him. I had no idea what to do or where to go, but God, unseen to me, was establishing my steps.

I can rest assured that God's plan will come to fruition. I may never understand the methods He chooses to enact His plans. I may never understand why such deep sorrow had to be part of my life at this time. I may not even understand where God is leading me. But I know that God *is* leading me, that He has a plan for my future, and that He has given me hope.

God is establishing my steps. I simply need to walk them.

PRAYER

Lord, let me cling to Your plan for my life. Let me not be afraid, for You are trustworthy.

MEDITATION

But the plans of the LORD stand firm forever, the purposes of his heart through all generations. (Psalm 33:11)

Many are the plans in a person's heart, but it is the LORD's purpose that prevails. (Proverbs 19:21)

thoughts to remember

FINDING HOPE IN THE DARKNESS

Under Each Roof

I sit on my patio on a beautiful late summer afternoon. A gentle breeze stirs the leaves while the birds make sweet chirps and tweets. The sky is deep blue and filled with billowy white clouds. The garden's color is waning, but flowers still dot the backyard. All I can think is, "It shouldn't be like this."

The chair next to me is empty. Once filled with Mark's large frame and generous smile, it sits unoccupied, covered in cobwebs. Although I hear lawnmowers in the distance and the mail truck as it rumbles by, it is too quiet. Mark's unique laugh does not split the silence. Even if Mark and I were not talking, we were still wordlessly communicating our thoughts by looks or body language. It is too empty, too quiet, too without him. He is thoroughly absent from my world.

I look at the houses around me. Next door is the widow who lost her husband to cancer. Down the street is the woman whose husband died from a brain tumor. Across the street is the single woman with her daughter. I look at each house and wonder what is going on beneath each roof. Is there pain there? And if it is not there today, will it arrive tomorrow?

It seems like everyone I talk to knows some kind of sorrow or grief. A mom with a special needs child. A dad whose son was murdered. A couple whose young daughter committed suicide. Deep, deep sorrow is etched on their faces. They are pulled into this whirlpool of grief, and they struggle to not disappear beneath it. All I can say to them is, "I'm sorry."

Jesus experienced deep sorrow while on earth. Isaiah calls Him the "Man of Sorrows." Surely Jesus has words of comfort for those in pain.

> *I have told you these things, so that in me you may have peace. In this world you will have trouble. But take heart! I have overcome the world.*
> *(John 16:33)*

Jesus never gave us a rosy picture of how life would be when we surrendered our lives to Him. He told us there would be trials and persecutions. Yet, He also told us that no matter what suffering we would go through, He would be there with us.

This is not an easy truth. We don't want Jesus with us in the pain. We want the pain to go away. There are days I tell God flat out—I don't want to do this anymore. But it is easier to float on the waves than fight against them. I must surrender to the will of God. Somehow, our pain and suffering draw us closer to the pain and suffering of Christ.

Every life will experience pain, suffering, disappointment, and grief. There is not a roof in my neighborhood that does not or will not have tears beneath it. The only way we can survive the storms of life is to cling to Jesus. He knows what our futures hold. He has overcome the pain and sorrow and even death of this life. He promises us a glorious future in heaven.

It shouldn't be like this, but it is. I take heart because it won't always be.

PRAYER

Lord, I thank You that I have Your promises to rely on for the rest of my life. You are trustworthy, faithful, and loyal, and You will not abandon me.

MEDITATION

"Though the mountains be shaken and the hills be removed, yet my unfailing love for you will not be shaken nor my covenant of peace be removed," says the LORD, who has compassion on you. (Isaiah 54:10)

Peace I leave with you; my peace I give you. I do not give to you as the world gives. Do not let your hearts be troubled and do not be afraid. (John 14:27)

thoughts to remember

FINDING HOPE IN THE DARKNESS

The Hole In My Heart

There is a gaping hole in my heart, a vast maw that threatens to swallow everything around me. It rumbles with sorrow and hideous wails of grief. It runs deep into my soul.

I want to run from it, hide from it. It torments me with thoughts of pulling me into its dark depths and holding me there forever. At times, it seems dormant. I can even function around its edges with some normalcy. I can look away and pretend it is not there.

But it is there, waiting for me. Ready to suck me into its profound blackness.

At times I try to avoid it. I try to sidestep that gaping hole with activities or people. I think that if I fill my time, the hole will shrink. Sometimes that works to distract me from the chasm, but distractions only last for a short time. To use people just to alleviate my pain is draining and hurtful to them. Eventually, nothing can distract me from what lies in my path.

Sometimes I try to figure out my own way through it. If I go through enough counseling, if I attend enough groups, or if I volunteer enough, maybe I will close this gap forever.

Distractions are not necessarily a bad thing. I cannot live in the sight of deep pain continually, or I will lose my mind. Counseling and volunteering are also good ways to learn coping skills. However, I cannot fill the hole with those things. There is only one way to deal with this vast emptiness.

> *Jesus answered, "I am the way and the truth and the life. No one comes to the Father except through me." (John 14:6)*

I picture that cavernous hole in my mind. It fills my present and swallows my future. I will never be able to get around it. I will never be able to fill it. But then, Jesus steps in. He takes my hand and says, "Let Me lead you." I yearn to draw closer to Him instead of falling into my grief. Slowly, I notice an amazing thing happening. As I draw closer to Jesus, as I fill my life with His Word, as I take His hand where He leads me, the gaping hole appears to shrink. It will never disappear, but as God fills my life, the hole gets smaller. Someday, with Jesus by my side, I will be able to simply walk over it.

I know my loss will be with me for the rest of my life, but it doesn't have to consume me. While distractions and activities have their place, Jesus is the only way to safely navigate around this treacherous hole of grief.

PRAYER

Lord, as You increase in my life, my grief will decrease. Draw me nearer to You and help me fix my eyes on You.

MEDITATION

I will instruct you and teach you in the way you should go; I will counsel you with my loving eye on you. (Psalm 32:8)

Whether you turn to the right or to the left, your ears will hear a voice behind you, saying, "This is the way; walk in it." (Isaiah 30:21)

thoughts to remember

God's Word tells me I am wrapped in the arms of God. He will never let go.

FINDING HOPE IN THE DARKNESS

In His Arms

I am not sure how I will survive the winter this year. My husband was not only much larger than I and could easily envelop me in his arms, but he was also always thermally warmer. He never wore a winter coat—it made him too hot, even in 10-degree weather. He wore a short-sleeve shirt and shorts well into fall and in very early spring. I felt like I could see the heat waves rising from his body. In the coldest of nights, I could attach myself to him like a barnacle, and because he was such a deep sleeper, he would never wake up. I stayed toasty warm.

I know there are warm coats and boots, gloves and scarves that will protect me against the bitterly cold weather. They might warm my body, but they will never warm my heart. Being in Mark's arms brought warmth, yes, but it also brought the comfort and security I will never find in a pair of mittens.

I have been told that as a widow, I need to be more conscious of physical contact. I am supposed to seek out a hug a day, and if I can't find one, I should hug myself. Although I appreciate the idea, putting my arms around myself only brings a shiver to my core. And although friends hug me, they give more guarded hugs than what I received from my husband. The only hugs that come close are the uninhibited, enthusiastic hugs of small children.

I miss his strong arms, the hands that held mine. One cold New Year's Eve, we went to a very crowded restaurant and were told we could wait outside by the fireplace for our table, which would be ready in about two hours. We were prepared. We sat under a warm blanket by the fire and snuggled close. Of course, many people entering the restaurant had to comment on us, but that only made us warmer.

Now, the only arms I rest in are the arms of God. They can't make me warmer, they can't elicit comments from passersby, but I am most definitely embraced.

> *The eternal God is your refuge, and underneath are the everlasting arms.*
> *(Deuteronomy 33:27)*

God's Word tells me I am wrapped in the arms of God. He will never let go.

I think of more than just the comforting, strengthening arms of God. I imagine Jesus, arms opened wide on the cross in an embrace spanning humanity. That embrace was the most loving, redeeming embrace in history, one that called, loved, and forgave all at one time. Without Mark's embrace, I will be cold this winter. But without God's embrace, I would be dead for eternity.

As the days get colder, I am reminded of the warmth that Mark's love gave me. I am also reminded of the saving grace of God.

PRAYER

Lord, I am wrapped in Your embrace for eternity. I thank You for Your loving sacrifice and long for the day I can hug You face to face.

MEDITATION

My hand will sustain him; surely my arm will strengthen him. (Psalm 89:21)

With a mighty hand and outstretched arm; His love endures forever. (Psalm 136:12)

thoughts to remember

FINDING HOPE IN THE DARKNESS

Fully Known

It was as if my husband and I had a unique language. I never worried about whether or not he knew I was making a joke. He always laughed. We saw an unusual sight and thought the same thoughts. He knew what a look meant. He knew I was in pain when I grew very quiet. He could tell I was hungry by the look on my face. Both verbally and non-verbally, we spoke the same language.

I could trust his sense of style because it was the same as mine. We had the same tastes in food (no squash, please). We liked the same kind of movies. In many ways, the two truly became one.

Of course, no marriage is perfect. We didn't always agree on where to go to dinner or what color to paint the bedroom. Sometimes, because of tiredness or stress, we would misinterpret what the other was saying. There were times he completely misunderstood what I was trying to convey, and it caused great strife. Sometimes, I couldn't figure him out if my life depended on it.

But for almost thirty-five years, we kept trying. Every person wants to be fully known by their spouse. It would be wonderful if, when we get married, we receive the key to our spouse's thoughts and emotions that would allow us to understand every nuanced grunt and sigh. We don't. As much as we want to understand each other, we often can't.

Now, with my spouse gone, my special language is gone as well. No one understands my quiet pain or pouting hunger. No one understands the raised eyebrow or tip of the head. If I meet someone new, it is frustrating to try and translate what they are saying into something I can understand. They don't know me, and I don't know them. At times, I am not even sure it is worth trying.

My desire to be fully known and fully loved is not a bad thing. It is God-designed. Marriage was meant to be a mirror of my relationship with God—love, acceptance, intimacy. But as sin corrupted the world, it corrupted marriage. Instead of love, there is self-centeredness. Instead of acceptance, there is judgment. Instead of intimacy, there is self-love. God's design cannot be fully achieved in a broken world.

> *You have searched me, LORD, and you know me. You know when I sit and when I rise; you perceive my thoughts from afar. You discern my going out and my lying down; you are familiar with all my ways. Before a word is on my tongue you, LORD, know it completely. (Psalm 139:1–4)*

There is only one who can ever fully know me even better than I know myself. That person is God. I wanted to be known by my husband, but my humanity too often got in the way and prevented me from fulfilling God's design. But Jesus, fully God and fully man, has always fully known and fully loved me. The desire that cannot be fulfilled by another will always be completed with God. I cannot expect a man to accomplish what only God can do.

I loved my husband, and he loved me. We tried our best to get to know each other. But ultimately, it is only God who can ever fulfill my need to be fully known and fully loved.

PRAYER

Lord, I am an open book before You. You know me better than I know myself. I cling to You and know You fully know me.

MEDITATION

Search me, God, and know my heart; test me and know my anxious thoughts. (Psalm 139:23)

For now we see only a reflection as in a mirror; then we shall see face to face. Now I know in part; then I shall know fully, even as I am fully known. (1 Corinthians 13:12)

FINDING HOPE IN THE DARKNESS

thoughts to remember

FINDING HOPE IN THE DARKNESS

Deep Waters

Mark and I loved to go to the beach. The sound and smell of the ocean was the most stress-relieving, peaceful vacation spot for us. The feel of sand beneath my feet, the warm sun on my skin, everything about it brought refreshment to my heart.

We both loved the beach, but we each behaved differently there. Mark liked to spend hours in the sun, basting himself with sunscreen and turning on his towel like a rotisserie chicken to get evenly browned. I, on the other hand, knew there was no amount of SBF 60 in the world that could stop me from turning a blazing, painful red. I stayed under an umbrella and kept protective gear nearby.

We liked to walk on the beach. The feel of the cool sand on our feet after being in the hot summer air was almost luxurious. I liked to walk on the edge of the water but not go in it. Mark liked to dive in and swim out in the ocean until the waves carried him back to shore. When I was in water above my knees, I couldn't stop thinking of what was in the water with me—jellyfish, sharks, whales. My imagination ran off with me.

I could also imagine being entangled by some submerged terror and being dragged down into the ocean's dark depths, as though the kraken could reach a long tentacle all the way to shore and claim me. It was an irrational fear, I know. But the ocean can be mysterious, dark, and dangerous, so I kept close to shore.

When Mark died, I felt as if I had been plunged into the middle of the dark, frightful ocean. The waves crashed over me with shocking power; I was unable to breathe, gasping, sputtering, disoriented. I felt abandoned and hopeless. The ocean of grief threatened to destroy me.

> *He reached down from on high and took hold of me; he drew me out of deep waters. (Psalm 18:16)*

For many months, I struggled in the deep waters of grief and pain. Waves of sorrow crashed over me. Terrifying, irrational thoughts circled beneath me. I had no rescue. I sank deeper and deeper.

Slowly, I felt saving arms wrap around me, pulling me to shore. I was too exhausted to make any effort to save myself. I was incapable of bringing my head above the pounding waves. But I clung to God's Word, the one chance I knew could preserve my life. Day after day, I immersed myself in Scripture, and the waves of grief began to recede. I clung to God's promises, especially promises to widows and the lonely. The waves eased, and I found myself in shallower waters. Where once I was drowning in pain and sorrow, I was now protectively wrapped in the arms of my Savior.

I did not dramatically rise from deep water. It took time, patience, and trust. Just as I never realized the depths to which my grief could take me, I never understood the peace of total trust in God until I surrendered to Him.

Today, I walk on the beach again. Sometimes, the waves reach my knees. At other times, they only lap at my ankles. I no longer feel as if I am daily drowning in sorrow. God has lifted me from deep waters.

PRAYER

Lord, help me to recall Your saving arms pulling me safely to shore as I felt I was drowning in grief. I could not have saved myself. You were there for me.

MEDITATION

From the ends of the earth I call to you, I call as my heart grows faint; lead me to the rock that is higher than I. (Psalm 61:2)

When you pass through the waters, I will be with you; and when you pass through the rivers, they will not sweep over you. When you walk through the fire, you will not be burned; the flames will not set you ablaze. (Isaiah 43:2)

FINDING HOPE IN THE DARKNESS

thoughts to remember

FINDING HOPE IN THE DARKNESS

A New Song

Before Mark's death, I sang on the praise team at my church. I don't consider my voice particularly worthy of holding a microphone, but my church is very small, and the criterion for being on the praise team is saying "yes" when asked. I generally can sing on key, so it was a perfect match. I truly felt blessed to be able to watch the congregation worship the Lord in song. Of course, standing head and shoulders above most was my 6'4" husband. He was always one of the first to stand, clap, and praise the Lord wholeheartedly in song.

After he died, I could not sing. It took me weeks before I even felt strong enough to go back to church. The memories of worshipping together were too strong, and I could not contain my emotions. Eventually, I was able to sing most of the songs while sitting with the rest of the congregation. Fellow members asked me when I would rejoin the praise team. I could only tell them I would return when I could get through a set without crying. There was one contemporary song in particular that brought copious tears because I had sung it to Mark while he was dying.

I started to miss not being able to help lead worship. As a friend of mine told me, it is a gift from God to be able to assist God's people in public worship, and that there was no higher calling for a musician. I needed to return to the praise team.

I had fears I would start to sing and then break down crying in front of the congregation. Because we are very much a church family, I was reassured that if that were the case, I could simply sit down. Still, I had no desire to make a spectacle of myself and detract from worship.

The day arrived. I survived practice and was able to sing during the service with not even a sniffle.

He put a new song in my mouth, a hymn of praise to our God. Many will see and fear the LORD and put their trust in him. (Psalm 40:3)

There is much to be said for the "new normal" people must find when their spouses pass away. It is not a normal anyone wants, but it is necessary in order to continue living. It is the new normal of eating styles and times, grocery lists, new entertainment, and meals alone. The new normal of day-to-day activities. But I have found that the Lord has also given me a new song.

My worship will never be the same. Now, I think of worshipping with my husband in heaven who is standing, clapping, and singing with the angels. I feel a deeper capacity for the love of God, who is walking with me on this journey. I pray that others will see my worship, my new song, after having seen my grief. I pray that they also will find a new, deeper song for their Lord. ❀

PRAYER

Lord, continue to put new songs within my heart throughout this journey. Let me worship You with my whole being.

MEDITATION

By day the LORD directs his love, at night his song is with me—a prayer to the God of my life. (Psalm 42:8)

Those who go out weeping, carrying seed to sow, will return with songs of joy, carrying sheaves with them. (Psalm 126:6)

FINDING HOPE IN THE DARKNESS

thoughts to remember

> *God is worthy of our absolute trust, not only in this life but also in the next. He will never hurt us. He will never lie to us. He will, always and forever, love us.*

A Hit Or A Scam

I admit it. After months of loneliness and fueled by curiosity, I joined a Christian dating website. I joined with no expectations; it was just an interesting experiment. I had nothing invested in these people, so I had nothing to lose. I put my profile out there and waited.

To my surprise, I had quite a few hits in the first twenty-four hours. Most I was not interested in, but a few I was, so I decided to test the waters by returning their interest. One, in particular, seemed like a nice match. He was good-looking, intelligent, and a Christian. And *he* was interested in *me*.

One of the emotions I had been dealing with was the fear that I would be alone forever. Yes, I had friends, close friends. Yes, I knew that God would never leave me or forsake me. But there was comfort in sharing life with a man for the past thirty-four years and nine months, and I missed a male perspective and insights. I missed a male voice. I was flattered and pleased that so many men expressed an interest in me so quickly. It was extremely painful for me to post my picture online because that has always been my Achilles heel. I hate taking pictures and I will pick apart the minutest details. New times call for new attitudes, however, so I prepared for battle, posted my profile, and now I was reaping the benefits. Or was I?

I messaged my man of interest for a while, and he seemed friendly and gentlemanly. Then a message from the website popped up. He was removed because of violating the terms of the website by possibly misrepresenting himself or soliciting money. In fact, over the course of a day, the majority of the people who had expressed interest turned out to be fake profiles or scams.

At first, I felt foolish. How could I think that so many men would be interested in me? Even though I told myself my self-esteem would not be impacted, I felt my being was de-valued. I was nothing but a mark, a desperate widow to prey on. Then, I felt angry. How despicable people are to take advantage of those who are searching for a friend. How dare they look for the weakest, the most vulnerable, and pounce on them with promises of a bright and loving future? Finally, my thoughts turned back to God.

In the months since Mark's death, I had an abundance of scam phone calls. Calls that said I was going to be arrested by the local police because of errors on my tax return. (The Federal Government NEVER makes these kinds of calls.) Calls that said my computer had a virus and if I did not return the call, my personal data would be held hostage. Call after call of lies and deceit. And now, a website filled with people wanting to take advantage of me.

> *Some trust in chariots and some in horses, but we trust in the name of the LORD our God. (Psalm 20:7)*

There always have been and always will be scammers in the world. There are people who seem attractive and powerful who say they want to help us. But these people may want to take advantage of us and even hurt us. However, God is worthy of our absolute trust, not only in this life but also in the next. He will never hurt us. He will never lie to us. He will, always and forever, love us.

In this world, God tells us we are sheep among wolves. He warns us to be as shrewd as snakes and as innocent as doves. We need to balance our Christian love with common sense. Most of all, we need to realize who we are in Christ and how much He loves us. God will never, never scam us.

PRAYER

Lord, help me realize that You are worthy of absolute trust in every aspect of my life. Let me seek You above all else.

MEDITATION

Fear of man will prove to be a snare, but whoever trusts in the LORD is kept safe. (Proverbs 29:25)

Trust in the LORD forever, for the LORD, the LORD himself, is the Rock eternal. (Isaiah 26:4)

FINDING HOPE IN THE DARKNESS

thoughts to remember

FINDING HOPE IN THE DARKNESS

A Changing Landscape

There is no "other side" to grief. As I travel this journey, the terrain changes. I start in devastation, a vast desert with nothing but barren rocks. Eventually, I see some evidence of life, of growth. I move through changing vistas. Occasionally, I find springs of refreshment. I will journey in this land in some fashion until my last breath.

When I was first assaulted by the deep grief of my husband's death, I thought I could not survive. I felt as if a mountain had crushed my heart. Would I ever be able to dig through the rubble? I knew I had to move through the detritus to get through to the other side, or I would die.

But I quickly learned that this is a lifelong journey. As landscape changes as we physically travel, so the landscape of grief changes with every step I take. At first, my grief was devoid of any signs of life. It was a harsh desert, offering nothing but vast emptiness and unrelenting loneliness. There was no respite from the pounding grief. There was no direction to follow. Blinding pain assaulted me each day, and I felt the carnivorous winds of sorrow eat the flesh off my grieving bones. If I hadn't moved, I would have been consumed.

After a few months, the landscape changed. I found an oasis, a place where I could find others traveling a similar path. We could stop and offer each other a cup of cold water. There was purpose in our meeting. We supported each other when the winds grew unendurable. We gave each other advice on how to weather the brutal storms. After a time, we continued our journeys, better equipped because of the wisdom and vulnerability of others.

The landscape changed. I began to see patches of green and more signs of life. Not every day held despair. I began to see purpose in pain. I began to see how sorrow propelled me further into the embrace of God. There were glimmers of hope, flashes of promise. Sometimes they appeared, wraithlike, in the corner of my heart and then vanished rapidly. Sometimes, they were so close I felt I could reach out and touch them.

The journey continues. The landscape changes. I know the future will hold streams of refreshment, green meadows of peace. I know it is in front of me. I also know I can't sidestep the journey. As much as I want to transport myself to another place and time, I cannot. Every step I take is precious to the Lord because He put me on this path. He has promised to lead me every step of the way.

Your word is a lamp for my feet, a light on my path. (Psalm 119:105)

When I try to step off the path He has given me, it only causes me heartache and more sorrow. I try to peer into the darkness of the future, but I cannot see. He gives me light for one step at a time. If I saw the entire landscape laid out before me, I am sure I would be terrified of all the impending hills and valleys. In His wisdom, He gives us light only for each day's journey. Trust is built as we follow His path.

PRAYER

Lord, give me light for each day, one step at a time. Help me stay on the path You created for me.

MEDITATION

Show me your ways, LORD, teach me your paths. (Psalm 25:4)

The path of the righteous is level; you, the Upright One, make the way of the righteous smooth. (Isaiah 26:7)

FINDING HOPE IN THE DARKNESS

thoughts to remember

FINDING HOPE IN THE DARKNESS

The Empty Chair

Recently, a friend called to tell me she had four free tickets to a musical event. After trying unsuccessfully to find someone for the fourth seat, my friend, her husband, and I went downtown to the performance. The fourth seat would just be left vacant.

When we arrived at the box office, we were given four tickets. What we didn't realize was that two tickets were in one location, and two tickets were in another. My friend looked at me with horror as she imagined me sitting through the entire performance, by myself, next to an empty chair. She tried to insist that we switch seats during mid-performance, but I assured her I would be fine sitting alone.

As we took our seats, I surveyed the crowd. Most people were in couples. Some were in groups. I didn't see many people sitting alone. I thought of Mark and how we had attended many events like these. He would have been in the seat on the aisle so his long legs had room to stretch. I looked at the couple next to me, lovingly holding hands as Mark and I once did. Somehow, I felt him there, encouraging me, saying, "You can get through this."

It wasn't an accident this happened. I have tried to do more alone. I have tried to embrace my single status and have even gone to breakfast and lunch by myself. Here, God was providing another opportunity to practice peace and acceptance of my "new normal." Since I could see my friends across another row, I was not totally alone. But the empty seat next to me reminded me my husband was gone.

As much as I did not want to accept it initially, there is still life to be lived. There is food to be enjoyed, people to meet, music to be heard. There are the possibilities of today and the promises of tomorrow. Gently, lovingly, God gives me opportunities to step farther from deep grief.

> *But you are a chosen people, a royal priesthood, a holy nation, God's special possession, that you may declare the praises of him who called you out of darkness into his wonderful light. (1 Peter 2:9)*

I enjoyed the performance. It was thought-provoking as well as entertaining. Most importantly, I was not a puddle of tears sitting by myself next to an empty chair. I was enjoying life.

I am reminded how God guides our every step, how He orchestrates each breath we take into a beautiful symphony of praise to Him. Just as there is often dissonance in music, there are jarring, disruptive noises in life. There is peace in knowing God conducts the music of my life. He will bring harmony. Each day may have an empty chair, but He fills my heart with the song of His love. ❦

PRAYER

Lord, the empty chair next to me reminds me that my husband is with You, enjoying the glorious riches of heaven. As I walk this road on earth, let me hear Your beautiful song in my heart.

MEDITATION

The LORD your God is with you, the Mighty Warrior who saves. He will take great delight in you; in his love he will no longer rebuke you, but will rejoice over you with singing. (Zephaniah 3:17)

And we know that in all things God works for the good of those who love him, who have been called according to his purpose. (Romans 8:28)

FINDING HOPE IN THE DARKNESS

thoughts to remember

FINDING HOPE IN THE DARKNESS

Brokenhearted

I really thought I was doing well. I had gone through both group and private counseling. I journaled daily, recording my thoughts, prayers, cries for mercy, and thankful memories. The tears, although they did not stop, had slowed to a manageable amount. My emotions were more controlled. People I knew told me how well I was doing, what an inspiration I was to those who grieve. I led Bible studies. I counseled troubled women. I had it under control.

Of course, I really didn't.

One day, it all came crashing down. As the holidays approached, I found myself crying more often. I had more and more grief triggers. I felt the icicles of sorrow encase my heart once again, choking any warmth I thought I had achieved. It could have been the weather around me—increasingly cold and dark. It could have been the decorations that surrounded me through neighbors and friends. It could have been the bombardment of memories that surfaced with all the activity of the holidays. It could have been the sudden removal of a grief "buffer" I wasn't even aware existed. Whatever the reasons, I suddenly felt that any progress I had made in my grief journey was lost. I was back to square one, on the ground, begging God for mercy.

I knew that my grief would ebb and flow, that I would always have triggers and sorrowful moments. But I was not prepared for the intensity of my emotions. I could not cope. I had no idea how I was going to survive all that I would need to face in the coming weeks. I spiraled downward, ashamed that I had even once imagined I had made any progress.

I was reduced once again to fragmented, weeping prayers. I could not stop my profuse tears. I felt as if I was losing my sanity. I asked friends to pray for me often. I felt as though I could not connect with any comfort from God.

I found that only one prayer could calm my heart.

> *He heals the brokenhearted and binds up their wounds. (Psalm 147:3)*

Mark was gone. Nothing could bring him back. There was no one or no thing that could change the path I had to walk. I repeated this verse again and again and again. I felt alone, but God's Word told me I was not. I was brokenhearted, but God did not forget me. I was crushed, but God promised to save me. God would heal me. God would bind my wounds.

These are not easy days. They may get worse before they get better. But God is faithful, good, and trustworthy. I will not spend the rest of my life in this desolate, anguished place. I thought I had escaped, but find myself inconsolable once again. This does not surprise God. We will walk through these days together. We will weep together. And together, we will find to-morrow.

PRAYER

Lord, I am brokenhearted. You are the only path to my healing. Keep me closer than ever before as I trust You for each day.

MEDITATION

The LORD is close to the brokenhearted and saves those who are crushed in spirit. (Psalm 34:18)

My sacrifice, O God, is a broken spirit; a broken and contrite heart you, God, will not despise. (Psalm 51:17)

thoughts to remember

FINDING HOPE IN THE DARKNESS

The Confidence Of God

It is hard for me to imagine what life would have been like had Mark lived. My world, as I knew it, disappeared when he died. His death impacted every habit, every food choice, every leisure-time activity. My future as I dreamed it died, but my today was also dramatically changed.

God took me apart, shattered me in one swift blow. I had never experienced such deep pain and sorrow. I didn't think I would survive, but I did. I still breathe the earth's air every day. I have found purpose. I even admit to seeing a future.

You would think that is enough, that God taking my husband would be more than enough change at one time. God has revealed many hard truths as I have walked this difficult, lonely road. He has drawn me nearer to Him. But God didn't stop there. He is still dismantling me, emotion by emotion, insecurity by insecurity, better forming me into an image of Him.

I am experiencing struggles I would never know were I still married. I struggle with how I look not matching the world's standards. God says I should be transformed by the renewing of my mind. I struggle with the overpowering loneliness that causes me to seek man above God, while God says I should seek His kingdom above all else. Most of all, I struggle with trusting God with my heart.

There is a part of me that says, "God took my husband; how can I trust Him again?" But my marriage is gone, Mark is gone, and I can only look to God for the emotional intimacy I so desire. And God is more than willing to give it.

> *The LORD confides in those who fear him; he makes his covenant known to them. (Psalm 25:14)*

I was astonished by this verse. I had been crying to God for emotional intimacy, for a heart connected with another human being. Here was God telling me, "I will show you my heart. I will confide in you."

The God of the universe desires to confide in me? To reveal Himself to me? To open His heart to me? To *me?*

I don't feel as though I have a lot of baggage to carry into a new relationship, but I do have some carry-ons. I have to find someone willing to be patient with me as I unpack these bags—someone who might actually see potential in getting to know me. But God is already here. He is unfathomably patient and grace-giving. He sees value in me and loves me, just as I am, more than I can possibly imagine. God is the ultimate heart connection. He wants to comfort me. He wants to love me. To cherish me.

I can never understand this connection with God. If Mark were still alive, I am not sure I would have ever pursued it. I am humbled and awed that God Almighty desires intimacy with me.

God continues to heal my heart, to take me apart, and to show me perfect love. God, being willing to confide in me, gives me the freedom to be completely vulnerable to Him, and to love others in the world with freedom and confidence.

PRAYER

Lord, I am humbled and awed by You desiring intimate fellowship with me. Help me trust You more each day, and the intimacy between us will grow.

MEDITATION

One who has unreliable friends soon comes to ruin, but there is a friend who sticks closer than a brother. (Proverbs 18:24)

Then you will know the truth, and the truth will set you free. (John 8:32)

FINDING HOPE IN THE DARKNESS

thoughts to remember

> *Can I, with outstretched arms and feet off the ground, cast myself into the arms of God?*

FINDING HOPE IN THE DARKNESS

Wild Abandon

A phrase originated by Dante in the *Divine Comedy* and borrowed heavily by pirates is, "Abandon all hope, ye who enter here." I felt as though I was living a pirate fantasy. My dreams were dashed, my treasure stolen. The one thing in life I held most dear was taken from me. I was close to abandoning hope.

One of the greatest joys in the midst of my grief is a friend's grand-daughter, little Indy. Even in my deepest sorrow, she can bring a smile. Once, while I sat on the couch, she got a sly look in her eyes and came running at me full speed from the other end of the room. With arms fully extended and feet off the ground, she launched herself into my arms like a flying mini super-hero. We laughed and giggled as I safely caught her. Then, she did it again. And again. And *again.* Each time, her body was stretched out while flying into my open arms. Each time, I caught her. She flew at me with complete and total abandon, and each time, I did not disappoint. Indy never once doubted I would catch her.

Little children were often brought to Jesus. He never turned them away, for He saw the innocent lack of constraint in their hearts.

> *Jesus said, "Let the little children come to me, and do not hinder them, for the kingdom of heaven belongs to such as these." (Matthew 19:14)*

I thought of how I desire that complete trust and abandon with God. I have a great example in Indy. But there is an even greater example of unrestrained trust.

When Jesus came to earth, He came as fully man and fully God. To be honest, I can't grasp the entire scope of that sacrifice. He came in obedience to the will of the Father. He came with arms outstretched. He came with reckless abandon.

As God, Jesus could see the final outcome—redemption for mankind from their sins. Salvation on an eternal scale. As man, Jesus must have weighed the cost. There would be sorrow and rejection. There would be pain and death, suffering to an unimaginable extent. Yet, trusting the arms of His Father, He flung Himself into our world, embracing all it offered. He was willing and obedient to abandon all that heaven held for the trials and pain of earth. Jesus modeled perfect trust and perfect abandon.

I face some days with trepidation. What will they hold? God is calling me in a direction I have never gone before. I trust God with my life, but can I abandon myself to His will? Abandoning myself means to completely give up my way of thinking, relinquishing all I once held fast in my hands, recklessly yielding myself to the will of God. Can I, with outstretched arms and feet off the ground, cast myself into the arms of God?

God is leading me down paths I never even knew existed. I am being stretched and formed to His likeness. He is asking me to be vulnerable and open to what the future holds. Instead of saying, "Abandon hope," He is saying, "Abandon yourself." He is waiting with open arms to catch me. I need only to fling myself to Him.

PRAYER

Lord, I fling myself into Your open, loving arms with total disregard for what I leave behind. I come to You as a child, with wild abandon.

MEDITATION

And call on me in the day of trouble; I will deliver you, and you will honor me. (Psalm 50:15)

Come to me, all you who are weary and burdened, and I will give you rest. (Matthew 11:28)

FINDING HOPE IN THE DARKNESS

thoughts to remember

FINDING HOPE IN THE DARKNESS

Open Hands

Grip strength is not my strong suit. My hands cannot hold on to objects as tightly as I once could. Rock climbing is now totally out of the picture. Even opening jars presents problems. However, in some ways, I grip too tightly on to things the Lord wants me to let go.

Babies display a reflex called the *palmar grasp*. Their fingers curl around any object that brushes their palms with a grip strong enough to support their body weight. I sometimes feel I am reflexively grasping on to things of this world. Something will enter my life, whether it be finances, material possessions, opportunities, or relationships, and I will close my fist with all my might. I don't want to let it go. The problem with the palmar grasp, however, is that it's unpredictable. At any moment, the grip could release, and the baby, if not otherwise supported, could fall.

My grip on the world is tenuous as well. At any moment, my finances may crumble, my possessions may vanish, my opportunities may fail, and my relationships may disappear. My life cannot depend on my hold. I must depend on the one who holds me.

This grief journey will continue for the rest of my life, although the path leads in different directions almost daily. I need to travel this road with open hands, not grasping on to the things I think I need. The Lord establishes my steps, and I must trust Him to provide for my journey.

I think loneliness is my greatest challenge. I need to be known by someone, to feel an emotional connection with another human being. Even to feel loved. As these things may pass my way, I grasp them with terrifying strength. I do not want to let them go. I pursue them to fill my lonely days and nights. These things are not bad in themselves, but if I grasp them to the point of holding them beyond what the will of God may be, I have a problem.

God says, "Open your hands. I will fill them."

That is the key. I can't think that I will remain empty and lonely for the rest of my life unless I grasp the things I think I need. If I open my hands and heart to be filled by God, I will receive what I *actually* need, not what I *think* I need. I will have no desire to grasp on to things of this world because I can rest assured that God will provide for all my needs. If my hands close on anything, it must be the hands of God.

> *I cling to you; your right hand upholds me. (Psalm 63:8)*

God has promised to hold me, to lead me, to provide for me, to love me for eternity. Nothing I could possibly grasp in this world could ever come close to His promises. I need only to release my grip on the things of this world and open my hands to Him.

As I cling to God, He will support me.

PRAYER

Lord, I walk this road with open hands. I release all to which I have been clinging. Fill my hand and my heart with Your love.

MEDITATION

Therefore, I urge you, brothers and sisters, in view of God's mercy, to offer your bodies as a living sacrifice, holy and pleasing to God—this is your true and proper worship. (Romans 12:1)

Come near to God and he will come near to you. (James 4:8)

thoughts to remember

FINDING HOPE IN THE DARKNESS

In The Garden

Grief will always be a part of me, hanging in my peripheral vision, not always seen, but able to swing into full view at a moment's notice. I try to keep it to the side so I can function in my daily life. Sometimes, it slips forward. I hear a song that triggers a memory. I see a shirt that Mark owned, but Mark is not wearing it. Simple things make grief slide forward.

We are nearing the Christmas season, and suddenly, the grief that was kept neatly to the side has swung into full view. It covers my face, and I see every scene, every person through the eyes of grief once more. Copious tears fill my days and, especially, my nights again. I thought I had moved aside some of this deep, deep grief that plagued my soul. Now it is back, and I can't escape it.

Scripture says we share in the suffering of Christ so that through Christ, our comfort overflows (2 Corinthians 1:5). During this season, my grief grew so great that I didn't want to live. Where could I find the comfort of Christ?

> *He took Peter, James and John along with him, and he began to be deeply distressed and troubled. "My soul is overwhelmed with sorrow to the point of death," he said to them. "Stay here and keep watch." Going a little farther, he fell to the ground and prayed that if possible the hour might pass from him. "Abba, Father," he said, "everything is possible for you. Take this cup from me. Yet not what I will, but what you will."*
> *(Mark 14:33–36)*

As I sat in my family room with tears streaming down my face, I thought of Jesus in the Garden of Gethsemane. Jesus went to pray, and being in great distress and sorrow, brought friends with Him.

How many friends have I asked to pray with me in my sorrow? There have been many, and my closest ones stayed near me in the worst of times. Their prayers and physical presence have surely sustained me in the many moments I thought I would lose my mind. But they are human, with human limitations, and my grief can drain them.

In the Garden, Jesus felt overwhelming sorrow. He even felt as if He would die from the weight of the grief. He fell to the ground and prayed for mercy, mercy that the trial would pass from Him.

Again and again I have been on the ground, pleading, begging God to take this sorrow from me. God could have done it. He could have lifted my heartbreak. He could have miraculously healed my heart. He could have changed my circumstances. Anything is possible with God. Yet, not what I willed, but what God willed.

I am sure there could be a less painful alternative to the grief I felt, but God, in His infinite wisdom, did not show me an easier path. He led me directly through the most difficult time of the most difficult time. I know my pain is somehow part of my healing.

The cup of suffering did not pass from Jesus. I cannot imagine how deep and overwhelming His sorrow was. The cup of suffering did not pass from me, either. Of course, Jesus drank His cup alone, knowing His Father would forsake Him in His hour of greatest need. But Jesus was able to look past the cross, past the most unimaginable, torturous suffering ever known, to see eternal glory.

God passed a cup of suffering to me, but I do not drink it alone. Jesus is with me, encouraging me, drinking with me, crying tears for each one of my tears. Jesus understands my distress so overwhelming I want to die. Jesus made it possible that I will never be alone in my grief. Jesus holds the gates of eternal glory wide open.

Sometimes, it is difficult to think of these things that occurred thousands of years ago and apply them to the intense pain and sorrow I am feeling at this moment. But God's love transcends time and space. Jesus, on the cross, thought of me in my family room, covered in tears, begging for God's mercy. Jesus, on the cross, made God's mercy possible.

Grief will always be with me, especially during holiday seasons. I can push it to the side, but I can never escape it. But when it swings fully to the front, I don't have to keep looking through the eyes of grief. I can, instead, see the world through the Father's love. ✿

PRAYER

Lord, it is with incredible love and humility that I think of You in the Garden, praying an agonizing prayer because of me. You understand my pain. You experience my sorrow.

MEDITATION

Surely he took up our pain and bore our suffering, yet we considered him punished by God, stricken by him, and afflicted. (Isaiah 53:4)

For we do not have a high priest who is unable to empathize with our weaknesses, but we have one who has been tempted in every way, just as we are – yet he did not sin. (Hebrews 4:15)

thoughts to remember

FINDING HOPE IN THE DARKNESS

FINDING HOPE IN THE DARKNESS

He Doesn't Let Up

There are days when my heart breaks anew. For the most part, I do not cry as often or as deeply as I did when Mark first passed away. But I still have days when I can't seem to get out from under the torrent of grief and pain.

I have done some difficult, grueling grief work. I determined that my loss would not define me, nor would I succumb to continual sorrow while ignoring the unconditional, everlasting love of God. I fought to dry my tears and allow God to heal my heart. And He did. So why do I still feel pain?

God is not subject to time and space, but I am. He could move me out of this place of grief and drop me in a place of no more suffering. He has, in ages past, suspended the sun in the sky, parted deep waters, rained fire from heaven. Moving my heart to a place without pain seems like an easy task for an omnipotent God. Why does He not do it?

My grief, although changed, continues. After all I have been through, I would think God would leave me alone and let me grieve in peace. But He does not. He shattered my soul as if it were glass, and now, being Redeemer, has taken the broken pieces and is using them to rebuild my life. He is reconstructing my soul to more closely resemble Jesus. He is banishing fear and insecurity in my life by making me face them head-on and choosing to acknowledge them. He is bringing up shame and guilt from the darkest, deepest places in my heart, not to torment me with them, but to heal me from them. He is making me trust Him by pulling the foundation from beneath me and allowing me to fall into His loving, always present, never failing arms.

He has taken me through deep waters. Now, He is leading me through treacherous terrain.

I will never understand why Mark was taken and I remain. Surely, Mark had the easier part. I now have to traverse this minefield of life, not alone, but clinging desperately to a hand I cannot see or feel but I know exists. The hand of God.

At times, I want God to leave me alone. I want to deal with my grief and find the oasis in the long journey. I want to find a happily-ever-after. But God has other plans. Again and again, I face fear and insecurity, shame and guilt, mistrust and doubt. Someday, *someday*, they will no longer have power over me.

I am definitely not the same person I was when I began this journey. I do not know where God is leading me, but of this I have no doubt: He *is* leading me. God did not leave me here to be swallowed by grief. He wants me to fling myself to Him, to trust Him with my whole heart and soul.

> *Cast all your anxiety on him because he cares for you. (1 Peter 5:7)*

Yes, God is polishing the jagged edges of my grief. But He also wants to polish the jagged edges of me.

At times, I feel God is sandblasting my soul, and the medium He is using is sorrow and pain. What will be left, if I allow Him to work, is His new creation.

I face these challenges knowing I cannot fight them. I am not strong or brave. God allows the battles of my heart so that He can fight them for me and show me the vastness of His love.

PRAYER

Lord, at times I don't want You to work anymore in my life. It is too painful. I can't take any more. Please calm my heart and remind me that You are good, faithful and trustworthy, and You are always acting in love.

MEDITATION

Those who know your name trust in you, for you, LORD, have never forsaken those who seek you. (Psalm 9:10)

For the LORD God is a sun and shield; the LORD bestows favor and honor; no good thing does he withhold from those whose walk is blameless. (Psalm 84:11)

FINDING HOPE IN THE DARKNESS

thoughts to remember

FINDING HOPE IN THE DARKNESS

Transplant

After all that has happened—coming in and out of the shadow of grief, dodging the winds of sorrow, and enduring unrelenting rains of pain—I could easily shut down my heart. The thought of opening myself to another, to unseal the closed places of my heart that have been scarred and battered, is utterly unpalatable. I have suffered enough. I will not do this again.

Although I know the character of God is good and holy and loving and faithful and trustworthy, even though I know God cannot be anything but what His character is, even though I know God does not change, my heart screams not to trust Him. I have been bruised and battered to the point where my soul is unrecognizable. I want to give up, to surrender the fight and cocoon myself so I will never be hurt again, by man or God.

My mind knows God would never allow me pain without purpose, but I am simply through with heartache. I cannot cry another tear. I cannot whisper another prayer for mercy. I cannot go on.

There are many, many promises about God bearing our suffering and carrying our pain. And I believe God's Word is truth. Why then, are there still tears in my eyes? Why does my heart ache so with disappointment and loss?

Certainly, after Mark died, my heart turned to stone. I could not bear the intensity and depth of grief. I did not want to live but prayed that God would take me so I would not have to endure this suffering another moment. My love for others turned cold. I loved my husband; how could I now possibly continue to love others with any measure of feeling?

Then God told me, gently and quietly, to open my heart. I did, slightly at first, and then with full unfolding. I felt hope and promise. I saw a future where the sun was shining once again. However, my circumstances changed, and as I took my eyes off the Lord, I felt as if everything fell apart. I was emotionally crushed. Again.

How could this happen? Did God truly allow even more grief and suffering in my life? Was it even possible for my heart to shatter more than it already had? Would I ever be able to love and trust again?

> *I will give them an undivided heart and put a new spirit in them; I will remove from them their heart of stone and give them a heart of flesh. (Ezekiel 11:19)*

God's ways are not our ways, as Job certainly knew well. Sorrow after sorrow fell upon Job, and yet he praised God. I will never have answers this side of eternity for what happens in my life. I still cry great tears that flow down my cheeks and wet my shirt and threaten to wash me away. But God's purpose in allowing pain is never to allow me to harden my heart. He takes from me my heart of stone and performs a spiritual transplant. The heart of stone is replaced with a heart of flesh. And unfortunately, while stone cannot feel, flesh can. God calls me to emotions and connections and love, knowing that there will be pain and sorrow. God is prepared to weep with me. But He will not cause me to turn my heart to stone, even though that is exactly what I want to do when the pain is so great.

I must trust God with my heart of flesh. He created me to feel pain and sorrow, love and joy. I cannot experience one without being vulnerable to the other. I must trust Him to lead me forward with my heart of flesh and to continue to love as He first loved me.

PRAYER

Lord, although I want to turn my heart to stone so I will not feel more pain and sorrow, You have put in me a heart of flesh. Let me use it to love others, as You would have me love them.

MEDITATION

I will give them a heart to know me, that I am the LORD. They will be my people, and I will be their God, for they will return to me with all their heart. (Jeremiah 24:7)

Jesus replied: "Love the Lord your God with all your heart and with all your soul and with all your mind." (Matthew 22:37)

thoughts to remember

> *There was victory in the cross, the horrific, beautiful cross.*

A Sanitized Cross

I would have never made it as a pioneer. I like my sanitized world. I like my grocery stores filled with pre-packaged meat—meat I did not have to butcher myself. I would surely starve if I had to chop the head off a chicken before I cook it.

Yet, I have no problem eating chicken. It comes home with me on a Styrofoam tray, wrapped in plastic. It has been cleaned and prepped and is ready for me to use in a recipe of my choice. I don't like to think of how that chicken got there.

I am on a grief journey. It is difficult and messy. The lessons I am learning are not easy, and there are times I would rather starve spiritually than actually be fed. I do not have a choice. I move forward, propelled by the work of Jesus on the cross.

I don't want to think about the cross. I know that I am saved by the blood of Jesus, that I have been transformed, that my eternity is secure because of what He did for me. But I don't want to think about how I got here. I don't want to think about the trials, the suffering, the violence Jesus endured for me. The thought is too horrifying. The reality of the crucifixion too devastating. I don't want to believe that my sins were so heinous that the Son of God had to die a torturous death on a cross, forsaken of God, so my sins would be forgiven.

I want a sanitized cross.

I want to remember Jesus's ministry, how He healed the sick and loved the unlovely. I want to quote His words of encouragement and hope. But I want to avoid the cross. I want to forget the torture and execution of an innocent, holy man. I just want Jesus to love me.

But the cross *is* His ultimate expression of love for me.

It is a hard truth that suffering often brings growth, and knowledge is often accompanied by pain. In the case of the cross, Jesus experienced all those sickening, gruesome things in my place. Now, God is asking me to travel my own path of grief. I do not want to acknowledge the pain, the suffering. I do not want to think about how I got here. Much like Peter rebuked Jesus for speaking of His death, I rebuked the Lord for making me travel this difficult road.

Peter and I both were wrong.

> *But he was pierced for our transgressions, he was crushed for our iniquities; the punishment that brought us peace was on him, and by his wounds we are healed. (Isaiah 53:5)*

Jesus's death was God's plan of salvation for us. Nothing else could accomplish this truth. This grief journey is God's plan for me. Although I don't understand why, God, in His loving omniscience, knows that this is the path I must travel. I know that it will lead to my good and His glory.

There was victory in the cross, the horrific, beautiful cross. There will be victory in my grief journey. I need to see it as it is: unsanitized, painful, but directed by God.

PRAYER

Lord, let the cross be ever before me as I travel this difficult road. Remind me of Your unimaginable sacrifice and Your eternal love for me.

MEDITATION

Then Jesus said to his disciples, "Whoever wants to be my disciple must deny themselves and take up their cross and follow me." (Matthew 16:24)

Fixing our eyes on Jesus, the pioneer and perfecter of faith. For the joy set before him he endured the cross, scorning its shame, and sat down at the right hand of the throne of God. (Hebrews 12:2)

thoughts to remember

FINDING HOPE IN THE DARKNESS

He Is Enough

After Mark died, I could barely pray. I mostly made animal-like noises, sobbed, and simply whimpered, "Mercy, Lord." The pain was overwhelming, all-consuming, a beast that threatened to devour me. Even the thought of survival hurt.

I moved through my grief, an ever-changing journey. Some days, I could distract myself enough to function. Some days, I simply sat on my couch and cried. God was with me on both the good days and the bad days. He taught me not to live in my emotions but to trust in His Word. I looked up specific emotions in the Bible to see what God had to say. I meditated on His precious words to me.

Anxiety: When anxiety was great within me, your consolation brought me joy (Psalm 94:19).

Discomfort: My comfort in my suffering is this: Your promise preserves my life (Psalm 119:50).

Loss: You're blessed when you feel you've lost what is most dear to you. Only then can you be embraced by the One most dear to you (Matthew 5:4 MSG).

Confusion: For God is not a God of confusion but of peace (1 Corinthians 14:33 ESV).

I looked up verse after verse on being directionless, on rejection, on sorrow and grief, on loneliness, on mercy. Especially mercy.

> *Be merciful to me, LORD, for I am in distress; my eyes grow weak with sorrow, my soul and body with grief. (Psalm 31:9)*

I always came back to the original cry of my heart for mercy. Yes, God showed me mercy, but in unexpected ways.

I desperately did not want to be alone. I wanted someone with whom to share my life. But mercifully, God did not answer that prayer. If He had, I would have looked more to a man for happiness, for my future, than to God. Instead, although my heart was broken and I felt sorrow upon sorrow, the shattered dream only made me realize that healing, happiness, and my future come only from God.

The pain was multiplied as I watched my prayer go unanswered. But more pain brought me even closer to my God. He was before me day and night, and I cried to Him for healing, for survival, for surrender, for His will to be done.

My pain became God's mercy because it taught me more about Him, about His faithfulness. It taught me about joy in the midst of crushing heartache and utter dependence on His Word.

The pain is great, and it is only God who sustains me in it. My heart is broken, but He promises to bind up my wounds. The broken places in my heart and the gaping holes left by grief only allow more spaces for His love to flow into me.

I pray someday I can reach past the grief and the tears, the pain and the sorrow, the confusion and the broken heart, and find that God, in His mercy, has shown me that He is enough.

PRAYER

Lord, there are days I feel I have lost everything in the world that is dear to me. I feel I will never be loved again. But Your Word, Lord, tells me again and again, I am loved completely and forever. Show me deep in my heart that You are enough.

MEDITATION

The name of the LORD is a fortified tower; the righteous run to it and are safe. (Proverbs 18:10)

And my God will meet all your needs according to the riches of his glory in Christ Jesus. (Philippians 4:19)

thoughts to remember

FINDING HOPE IN THE DARKNESS

The Journey

As I look back over the last few months, I am filled with gratitude to God for walking me through them. Of course, my journey is nowhere near complete. I have many days before me, God willing, and no doubt there will be days filled with pain and sorrow. But God is faithful. He did not leave me alone in the deep waters of grief. He swam by my side.

There were many practical measures I took to work out my grief. Almost immediately, I began to write in my journal. I found this extremely helpful in processing my emotions. Even though my first entries are almost indecipherable, I can read the pain in them. God didn't care what I wrote. I was simply crying out to Him.

I joined an exercise class, which had many benefits. It gave me a place to go in the morning, it helped me make friends, it allowed me to release some of the physical stress I felt. I joined a Bible study class, and although I could not fully focus on what was being discussed, I was around other women and felt their love and support. Eventually, I even led the class in a study on disappointment. Bible study also helped to create a habit of daily reading and searching the depths of God's Word. I did word studies on loneliness, grief, and any other emotion that surfaced that day. I also read many books on grief and gleaned some very helpful advice and insight.

I found both group and private counseling to be very beneficial. Counseling helped me to stay honest with myself and to weigh the impact of my emotions versus the truth of God's Word.

Of course, I could not have survived without my friends. They made sure I ate and dressed, and even made sure I had entertainment. Most of all, they showed me unconditional love and grieved beside me. They wept with me and even sometimes laughed with me. But their presence alone meant the world.

I am still learning. The hardest lessons are still before me. Is God enough? Can I truly say I am content in the plans God has for me? What if I am alone the rest of my life? What if my heart's desire is never met? What if...

All of the measures I took are good, and I needed those distractions to keep me sane. But ultimately, they will not lead to my healing. My healing is Jesus Christ alone. He calls me His Beloved and loves me with an everlasting love. I pray that one day I can fully understand how He pursues me, how He cherishes me, how He is my Husband.

> *See what great love the Father has lavished on us, that we should be called children of God! (1 John 3:1)*

Yes, God is enough, even on the days I don't feel like He is. Thankfully, my feelings don't stop Him from embracing me daily and covering me in His love.

PRAYER

Lord, I cannot thank You enough for Your love. You loved me enough to die for me. You will be my love forever.

MEDITATION

Therefore, since we have been justified through faith, we have peace with God through our Lord Jesus Christ, through whom we have gained access by faith into this grace in which we now stand. And we boast in the hope of the glory of God. (Romans 5:1-2)

We love because he first loved us. (1 John 4:19)

thoughts to remember

Epilogue

> *Jesus said to her, "I am the resurrection and the life. The one who believes*
> *in me will live, even though they die; and whoever lives by believing in*
> *me will never die. Do you believe this?" (John 11:25-26)*

I take great comfort in imagining Mark in heaven, a smile on his face and joy in his heart as he rests in the arms of his Savior, Jesus Christ. This is not merely in my imagination or one of my beliefs. This is the truth of God's Word.

Because Mark and I both accepted Jesus Christ's death on the cross as payment in full for our sins, I know for certain where he is now, and where I will be someday.

I cannot imagine not having this confidence in Christ.

If you do not know Jesus Christ in this personal, life-affirming, salvation-granting way, you can pray the following prayer:

Dear Jesus, I realize I am a sinner. There is no act I can ever perform or no prayer I can ever pray that would make me good enough for heaven. But I know that the blood You shed on the cross covers my sins completely. I accept Your sacrifice for me and ask You to forgive my sins and live in my heart, that I may live forever and worship You in paradise.

Please see my Facebook page @KarenPilarowski
for updates and more information

CPSIA information can be obtained
at www.ICGtesting.com
Printed in the USA
BVHW011140140421
604944BV00012B/60